—— LOST LINES: ——
WESTERN

NIGEL WELBOURN

IAN ALLAN *Publishing*

C O N T E N T S

First published 1994
Reprinted 2000

ISBN 0 7110 2278 X

© Nigel Welbourn 1994

Published by Ian Allan Publishing

an imprint of Ian Allan Publishing Ltd, Terminal House, Shepperton, Surrey TW17 8AS.
Printed by Ian Allan Printing Ltd, Riverdene Business Park, Hersham, Surrey KT12 4RG.

Code: 0011/2

ACKNOWLEDGEMENTS
I would like to thank all those who helped me with this book.
In particular, I would like to thank my parents whose patience and understanding when I was younger allowed me to visit so many lines that are now closed.
I would also like to thank all those courteous and helpful railwaymen and women who once worked on the lines mentioned in this book.

Nigel P. Welbourn DIP TP, DIP TS, MRTPI, FRGS.

Cover photographs: Colour-Rail

Introduction

The Western Region is the first book in the series 'The Lost Lines'. A cross-section of closed lines have been selected for this volume, for their regional interest and for their wider historical and geographical associations.

In 1923, by amalgamation of smaller companies, the railways of Great Britain were divided into the 'big four': the Great Western Railway, the London Midland and Scottish Railway, the London and North Eastern Railway and the Southern Railway. When these private companies were nationalised on 1 January 1948, the new organisation — called 'British Railways' — was divided into six regions for management purposes. A separate Western Region was established, the others being Scottish, London Midland, Southern, Eastern and North Eastern.

Although there had already been some closures, at their formation the six regions covered one of the most comprehensive railway networks in the world. Yet it was clear, even then, that the changing emphasis in economic and travel patterns was no longer reflected in the arrangement of lines. The problem was compounded in that after heavy World War 2 use, the equipment on many lines was life-expired. Thus it was that the railways at nationalisation had extensive arrears of both maintenance and investment.

The ever increasing inroads of the car and lorry meant that financially the railways were no longer in a particularly sound position and British Railways fell ever deeper into debt. As a consequence, in the 1960s notice was served that the complete railway network, which had survived relatively intact until that time, would be scrutinised as never before. The financial contribution of individual lines was to be examined and it was clear, from the somewhat stringent methods of accountancy, that many would be unlikely to survive on a purely commercial basis. In a surprisingly short time the system was reduced in size. By the 1970s, when the brake was eventually applied, about 8,000 miles of line had been lost, enough to equal the diameter of the world.

In the knowledge that change was inevitable, in the 1960s I started to record my travels by train and in the following years I eventually covered, with a few short exceptions, every passenger railway line on each of the six regions. The railway network is much smaller than when I first set out and the Western Region itself was abandoned after four decades of geographical division in favour of other means of organisation. My subsequent visits to lines closed show that much still survives. Indeed, the earthworks and structures of abandoned lines have their own fascination, lost to the present, but certainly not forgotten.

Below: Time was also running out for many branch lines in the 1960s. Regular passenger services ceased to Ashburton in November 1958. Ian Allan Library

1 Historical perspective

The Western Region (WR) had as its roots the Great Western Railway (GWR). This railway was authorised by an Act of Parliament in 1835 to link Bristol with London, and in that order. Isambard Kingdom Brunel (1806-59) was appointed as engineer. The word 'engineer' is derived from 'ingenious' which provides an apt description of his design of the line. His visionary broad 7ft ¼in gauge provided billiard table running conditions and set a precedent of speed for the Great Western Railway at that period. It was the first railway to bear the title 'Great' and stands today as a memorial to Brunel. Both terminals of the line at Bristol Temple Meads, with its creative hammer-beam styled roof, and at London Paddington, which at its opening was on a greenfield site, combined the ingenuity and flair of Brunel.

Unfortunately, one of the ill fortunes of railway history was that other railways were constructing lines largely to the 4ft 8½in standard gauge which had become well established. This meant that the Great Western's 7ft 0¼in gauge became increasingly separated from the rest of the system. In 1846 the government passed the Gauge Act frustrating any further use of broad gauge on new lines. The GWR realised that its future depended on collaboration with its standard gauge rivals. Whilst dual gauge had been used, by the addition of a third rail within the broader track, in 1892 the final broad gauge train left Paddington. The battle for broad gauge lines was lost.

The GWR recovered from this setback; it continued to absorb smaller companies, new lines were constructed to make the old routes more direct and in the locomotive department there was increased standardisation. The Great Western's centre for engine building was at Swindon, which became the greatest railway works of all time. Thus it was that the GWR

V. J. CORASI

Above left: GWR Coat of Arms: the design was simplified in later years, the company retaining only the central crests of Bristol and London, even after the system extended to many more cities. Ian Allan Library

Above right: Birmingham Snow Hill Station. An original drawing by V.J.Corasi

Left: Since 1982 a bronze statue of Isambard Kingdom Brunel sculpted by John Doubleday has sat on the concourse of Paddington Station, viewing his empire to the west. Author

became celebrated once again for some fast running trains on its main lines. The railway also had important freight traffic and one of the GWR's most resourceful developments was the port at Fishguard. This was opened in 1906 for Irish and, in its initial years, for transatlantic traffic. An equally important part of the GWR's freight activity was in the South Wales coalfield, though efforts in the 1920s to enhance efficiency by building 20 ton wagons failed; coal proprietors would not contribute to new loading facilities to provide for the wagons.

The GWR was the 'Holiday Line'. Its branches served the Devon and Cornwall coasts, which were promoted for their moderate weather and as all-the-year-round resorts with travel encouraged by naming trains such as the 'Cornish Riviera Express'.

Therefore, perhaps rather surprisingly when compared to some railway companies, the Great Western owned few hotels. Paddington was an exception. Hardwick's French Baroque style Great Western Railway (later GW Royal) Hotel, which on its opening was the largest hotel in the country, was incorporated into the station. The other main GWR-owned hotels were not originally built for the railway. They included the Tregenna Castle Hotel near St Ives, the Manor House Hotel near Moretonhampstead and the Fishguard Bay Hotel at Fishguard.

Out of the big four railway companies formed in 1923 the Great Western was the only one to retain its original title and most of its network, thereby holding on to much of its original individuality. As with the other railway companies established in 1923 the Great Western obtained road transport powers and had a financial holding in numerous bus operators within its territory. In fact it had about 300 buses on almost 170 services in the late 1920s. It was clear even then that the railway saw a future in road transport in many rural areas.

The GWR was good at public relations. Its employees were generally both smartly dressed and businesslike, even though in reality questions as to why a connecting branch train left just before the arrival of the main line train were sometimes answered with replies such as 'The Great Western Railway has its reasons.' It was none the less a resourceful railway that produced dividends for its shareholders until nationalisation.

Even on nationalisation in 1948 the newly formed Western Region retained its pre-Grouping identity more than most. This was because the Great Western Railway, which had operated under the same company name for over 100 years, had built up a remarkable corporate image that remains even today. The

design of everything, down to the smallest detail, was distinctive so you always knew from Snow Hill to Severn Beach that you were in GWR territory. Thus it was that the Western Region seemed to retain more or less the ambience and glamour of GWR for many years after that company ceased to exist.

A map of the Western Region in its early years showed little change from a map of the Great Western Railway. There were some reductions and changes, particularly in South Wales, but at first the WR maintained a network of about 3,800 route miles, the bulk of which was inherited from the GWR. Much of the style of the old company also continued. The region adopted brown as its colour which was more or less the GWR chocolate. The famous chocolate and cream main line carriage livery was maintained for a while and the ships still displayed the GWR coat of arms. The WR continued with the use of lower quadrant

Above: The Great Western Railway's monogram can still be found in many locations, such as this one prominently featured at the front of the Great Western Royal Hotel at Paddington Station in August 1993. *Author*

Left: The sad end of Swindon's 'A' Shop in February 1988. *R. E. Ruffell*

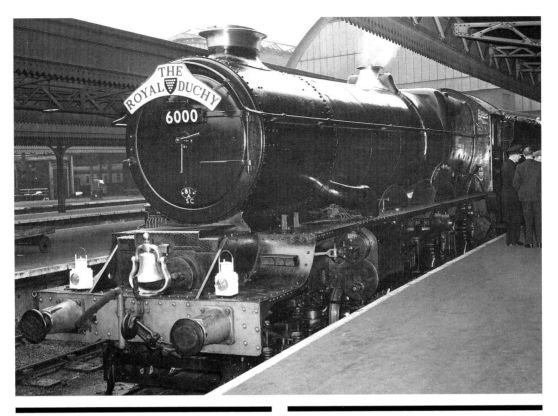

Above: A reminder of the extent of the system as No 6000 King George V awaits departure for Cornwall at Paddington station on 28 January 1957. The bell was a souvenir of its trip to the USA. *British Railways*

Below: Closures were not limited to small branch line stations; for a number of years after its complete closure in 1972 Snow Hill station in the centre of Birmingham remained in an ever increasing derelict condition. *Ian Allan Library*

Left: There were particulary extensive losses in South Wales. This view of Mountain Ash station on the Neath to Pontypool line was taken in March 1972. A. Muckley

Below: Time was running out for steam in the early 1960s and all of the 'Kings' were taken out of service by 1963. This shows a wheel modification to No 6023 King Edward II, nevertheless the engine survived and a replacement wheelset has been cast. G. P. Cooper

signals, even displacing some upper quadrant signals on lines it acquired from other companies. Indeed it was said that there were five regions of British Railways, and the Great Western.

Yet it was clear that many lines no longer reflected the patterns of freight and passenger movements through and within the region. There was a view that away from the Western Region's main lines, there was something to be said for hiring a car rather than using the network of slow and run down branch lines, many of which had long gaps both in new investment and in their timetables. In South Wales the absolute maze of lines, built originally by competing companies and serving a rapidly diminishing coalfield, was bound to contract for both freight and passengers.

From 1953 onwards British Railways fell increasingly into debt. In 1955 the WR had about 115,000 staff and by the early 1960s the region was responsible for about a third of BR's total loss. For years it had resisted change and standardisation, but in 1961 Dr Richard Beeching became Chairman of the then new British Railways Board. His mandate — to improve the financial circumstances of the railways — threw the sanctity of the WR to the wind.

On secondary routes there was little attempt to cut costs and win back lost traffic; closure was usually seen as an easier option. British Railways' first annual report recorded a total of 19,630 route miles; by 1970 this had been reduced to 11,799 miles, with much of the loss occurring in the period 1962-6. Moreover, closure came to involve more than withdrawal of train services, it usually meant removal and sale of track and equipment, the demolition or sale of property and an *ad hoc* approach to demolition of bridges and sale of land. The result was that any prospect of eventual reopening was made all the more difficult.

Change came with the 1968 Transport Act, which acknowledged the case for grant aid. In the 1970s and 1980s the value of retaining railways became increasingly recognised, together with the fact that closures did little to improve the railways' overall financial position. As a result, fewer and fewer lost lines were added to the list and by 1993 a total of 10,270 route miles remained.

What of the future? After four decades of geographical division, the six regions were abandoned as the principal means of organising the railways. Change is inevitable, but much of my professional time as a planner is spent looking at the future nature

of change. My own long term outlook is particularly optimistic for railways. Continued road growth is unlikely to be sustainable. I forecast that in the future many lost lines will be 'found' as a compelling means of relieving congestion and that even a number of lines outlined in this book could be reopened.

2 Geography of the region

The Western Region was primarily, as the name suggests, a region that covered the West of England. It fanned out like a river delta from London, but the network in the London district was limited compared to some regions. It served many of the less developed parts of the country, including large rural tracts in the South West, Wales and in the Welsh border counties. The exact area covered altered over the years, but in general terms the region extended from the Thames Valley and then stretched northwards to the Cheshire Plain. It included parts of the West Midlands, the Vale of Evesham and Central Wales. To the south its routes extended through Berkshire and Wiltshire into parts of Dorset, Somerset, Devon and Cornwall. The main line to Bristol proceeded below the Severn Estuary to serve South Wales.

Although Brunel was skilled at utilising the local topography to minimise engineering works required, the overall geography of the area covered by the region led to the construction of a number of world class engineering accomplishments, most of which are still in daily use. For many years the 4mile 628yd long Severn Tunnel was the longest underwater tunnel in the world. Box Tunnel is said to have been aligned to allow the sun to shine directly through it on Brunel's birthday. The flattest brick-arched bridges in the world cross the Thames at Maidenhead and are known locally as the 'sounding arches' because of the echoes produced by Brunel's perfect elliptical spans. In particular, Brunel's exceptional Royal Albert Bridge over the Tamar, the only railway-supporting suspension bridge in the world, remains virtually as originally constructed.

With some exceptions, the area covered by this book is broadly based on the Western Region boundary that was established on the nationalisation of Britain's railways in 1948. At that time the boundaries selected for the WR more closely fitted the old GWR than those finally arrived at after a number of alterations. The geographical area of the Western Region as it finally emerged lost much of North Wales and the West Midlands to the London Midland Region, but gained former Southern Region lines in the South West peninsula.

Above: Map of Regional Boundaries 1958. Ian Allan Library

③ The descending orders of freight

The transport of freight up to World War 2 was largely by rail. This was a period before road transport had made serious 'inroads' into the railway's freight trade and everything imaginable travelled by rail. The GWR built special wagons for fish, fruit and other perishable items. Glass-lined tank wagons transported milk to the capital and all sorts of livestock were carried by rail, usually in specially built rolling stock. A fleet of delivery vehicles transported the goods from the rail depot to their final destination. Equally as diverse as the freight itself were the freight handling facilities, ranging from huge depots and marshalling yards to single sidings.

At the top end of the scale the GWR had several large depots in the London area. Indeed the expansion of London itself has been much influenced by freight transport. The Romans built London at the point where the River Thames could be forded. Later development was associated with the river's tidal limit as sea-going vessels could reach the heart of the city. Main roads and then railways all converged on the capital. Originally the GWR served all of the London area with goods depots on its own lines and by travel-ling to its own freight depots over other railway companies' lines. The main goods depots were at Acton, Brentford (Town Station), Paddington, Park Royal and South Lambeth, whilst running powers were provided over other lines to Smithfield, which was connected directly to the meat market, and to the Victoria and Albert Docks in the East End. These depots together with others at Warwick Road, Chelsea, Hammersmith, Shepherds Bush, Westbourne Park and Old Oak Common allowed complete coverage of London, including areas far from traditional GWR territory.

The scale of the freight yards and depots was equally impressive. At Paddington the thirteen acre depot contained miles of sidings and was located to the north of the existing station on the site of the first 1838 passenger station. At its peak the depot dispatched over 30 freight trains a day, whilst around 700 horses and nearly 5,000 employees were associated with the depot in one way or another. The busiest time was at night, due largely to businesses conveying goods to the depot at the end of their working day, but assisted by the fact that lines were relatively clear

Below left: Just two of the eighty four Thornycroft 2 ton lorries supplied in the spring of 1934 to Paddington goods depot. Ian Allan Library

Right: A huge number of different types of wagons ran on specific routes, such as this one between Newton Abbot and Paddington and now preserved at the Didcot Railway Centre. Author

Below: The trolley method of working at Paddington Goods station in February 1968. British Railways

of passenger trains and consequently available for night freight trains. The depot was rebuilt in 1929, but after many years of decline the remaining facilities closed at the end of 1972 and the vast area of lines and associated buildings was gradually removed.

At the other end of the freight operation, remote rural areas were served by wagons to a particular section of line. Each was stored in a station siding or dedicated goods siding until loaded or unloaded. The wagons would then be collected by the 'pick up'

goods. In particular, many of the smaller stations served London and other cities with items such as fish, milk, meat, fruit and vegetables. Nationalisation saw a rationalisation of the competing companies' depots, followed by closures as traffic declined. With the exception of some specialised freight at Brentford and at Acton, none of the GWR depots mentioned is now open for freight. Equally, not all of closed depots had been fully redeveloped by 1994, including Paddington.

Left: The size of Paddington goods shed can be seen in perspective as this diesel multiple unit arrives on the suburban line in July 1970. J. Rickard

Below left: The vast span of unnecessary bridgework over the former freight lines out of Paddington in July 1993 gives a clue to the scale of freight that once used the station. Author

Above: The vast expanse of Paddington goods depot in July 1993. The overall roof has long since been removed, but the cobbles are a reminder of the traffic that was once generated in this area. Author

Below: One of the entrances and exits to Paddington goods yard which included a weighbridge. In July 1993 it led to a vast derelict area, although there are plans for redevelopment. The A40(M) Flyover can be seen in the background. Author

Above: Fishguard had no significant manufacturing industry, but until the end of the 1950s a brisk traffic in dead rabbits existed for the London and other markets. Myxomatosis put an end to the trade. J. E. Martin

Right: The ubiquitous 4-wheeled wagon abandoned at Sharpness Docks in June 1993. The unfitted short wheel-based wagon fell from grace and clearly this survivor has not seen service for some considerable time. Author.

Below: Loading broccoli at Ponsandane sidings near Penzance. This was just one of the thousands of sidings that fed into the system. R. C. Riley

4 Blewbury at war and peace

The Didcot, Newbury and Southampton Junction Railway (DN&SJR) provided a link from the GWR at Didcot to the London and South Western Railway (L&SWR) south of Winchester. The two established companies were concerned about this encroachment into their area. In particular the L&SWR would not co-operate and as a consequence the DN&SJR company decided to continue its own line to Southampton. However, finance was a problem and the line never reached the south coast. The first 18-mile section of line opened in April 1882 between Didcot and Newbury. This was followed by the 26¼ miles to Winchester which was opened in May 1885, whilst the L&SWR ultimately conceded to a junction with its line at Shawford, south of Winchester, which opened in October 1891.

The line was scenically interesting. Although looking direct on a small scale map, travelling south from Didcot was via a curving route that was forced to climb up the North Wessex Downs. The open landscape, however, was particularly attractive where the line ran between Blewbury Down and Churn Hill. The small unlit platform at Churn, some 7 miles south of Didcot, must have been one of the most isolated locations in the South East. In a foretaste of later health and safety regulations, trains called exclusively during

Above: Churn name board on this isolated platform in June 1957. Hugh Davies

Below: Collett 0-6-0 No 2214 near Whitchurch with the 2.12 pm Eastleigh to Newbury train on 31 July 1959. J. C. Beckett

daylight hours. Once having crossed over the ancient transport route of The Ridgeway the line passed through the rural villages of Compton and Hermitage to reach the expansive and typically GWR station at Newbury.

Crossing the GWR main line the route then continued southwards towards Winchester through attractive rolling Hampshire countryside, under the L&SWR main line to Salisbury at Whitchurch, where no connection was made, and on to Worthy Down where a connection with the main line to Southampton was first provided as a World War 2 measure. The line then continued via a tunnel to Winchester Chesil. With the original aim of proceeding independently to Southampton the line rather needlessly ran in a loop around the city, continuing south over an attractive viaduct directly west of Twyford Down to join the Southampton main line to the south of Winchester.

The line retained independence until 1923 when it

Above: Collett 0-6-0 No 2246 on a southbound local passenger train at Compton. The corrugated iron shed blocking the view of the platform was provided in 1927 and was used to store milk sent from nearby Barclays Farm.
D. Lawrence

Left: Collett 0-6-0 No 2240 sets off from Compton with a northbound train.
D. Hepburne-Scott

became part of the GWR and because of this association I include the entire route in this volume. It provided a direct route from the north to Southampton and as such it was seen as a vital diversionary line in the event of main lines being severed by enemy action in World War 2. This caused problems, as it was mainly a single line of limited capacity. The lengths of passing loops were not adequate to deal with wartime traffic and light bridge construction imposed limitations on axle loadings.

The only real solution was for the line to be closed to allow complete upgrading. Consequently for the period between 4 August 1942 and 8 March 1943 the train service was suspended with a substitute bus service being provided. The 18-mile single line section from Didcot to Newbury was doubled, together with the first 2 miles south of Newbury. The weight problems were solved by double-heading trains, but the difficulties posed by the passing loops not being able to accommodate the length of trains using the remaining single line sections were more exacting. The existing loops on the line were such that the

points could be physically worked by a central signalbox. Their extension meant that this was no longer possible. The solution was found in the use of electric points operated by a hand generator!

On nationalisation the route was divided into two regions, the Southern Region (SR) being in control south of Newbury. The preserved GWR locomotive *City of Truro* was removed by the WR from York Railway Museum in 1957. It was returned to working condition at Swindon and used on several occasions on this route, but the attraction of the *City of Truro* was insufficient to save the line. The SR section south of Newbury from Enborne Junction to Shawford was

the first to close during March 1960, although trains from Shawford to Winchester Chesil lasted until September 1961. The section from Newbury to Didcot closed the following year in September 1962.

After some lingering uncertainty as to whether the Didcot to Newbury section might one day be used again, the track for this section was also finally removed. For a number of months a demolition train left Didcot with wagons that were left in groups along the line. Sections of rail were removed and a caterpillar excavator tore up the sleepers. Each day a trainload of debris drew back to Didcot for unloading. The down line was the first to be removed, then it was the

Above: Gloucester single unit diesel railcar W55015 stands at Didcot in October 1960 with a Newbury train. This part of Didcot station was remodelled after closure of the line. *P. H. Wells*

Right: The overgrown location of Churn platform in June 1993. Freight ended on this section of line in August 1964. *Author*

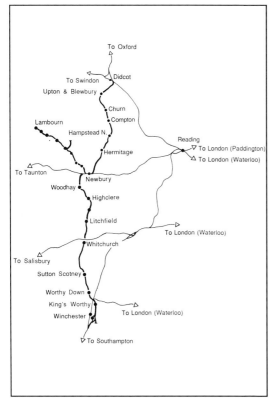

turn of the up line. Starting from Newbury the track was finally completely removed.

The line can still be traced for much of its route. An overgrown widening of the old route is a clear clue to the former existence of Churn platform. The more substantial station buildings on this line are of distinctive design and where retained are mainly in residential use. The station house at Compton is located with other properties in Beeching Close. Winchester and King's Worthy stations have been redeveloped. A section south of Newbury is to be used as the route of the Newbury bypass, while sections of the route in Hampshire are in use in conjunction with improvements to the A34 road.

Above right: Bridge over the line to the north of Churn in June 1993. Author

Right: Compton station sign and the sign from the signalbox preserved at Didcot Railway Centre, June 1993. Author

5 The valley of the racehorse

The Lambourn Valley runs in a north-westerly direction from Newbury where the River Lambourn joins the River Kennet. It was in this attractive valley, that wends its way up into the broad shoulder of the Lambourn Downs, that the Lambourn Valley Light Railway eventually opened its 12-mile line from Newbury to Lambourn in April 1898. This was a relatively remote area with perhaps more racehorses than potential passengers. The River Lambourn on occasions dries up and so did the railway's finances. As a consequence of the company's difficulties, its rolling stock was removed in 1904. Passenger traffic was transported in railcars loaned by the GWR until the line became part of that company the following year. In the 1930s the GWR employed a diesel railcar on the line. This was powerful enough to haul a

Right: 0-6-0PT (Pannier Tank engine) No 3740 with a branch passenger train for Newbury at Lambourn in May 1958.
D. Lawrence

Below: 0-6-0PT on the one coach up Lambourn valley branch train at Great Shefford in May 1958. Note the 'pagoda style' waiting room.
Hugh Davies

horsebox if necessary. The line was always a backwater. Newbury West Fields Halt, the first stop on the line, was closed in February 1957 and the whole line closed to passengers in January 1960, prior to the Beeching cuts. The line remained open as far as Welford Park for freight associated with a nearby United States Air Force military depot. As the junction faced the Lambourn direction, trains were obliged to reverse on to the military connection which rose out of the Lambourn Valley to the USAF depot. This remaining section was closed in November 1973 when the Western Region ran four special last trains for about 3,000 enthusiasts who wished to pay their final regards to the line.

After the closure, a campaign was launched to reopen the line. In particular it was seen as an opportunity to divert ammunition to the military depot off the local roads, but also to use the line as a tourist

attraction. However, it was asserted that the USAF could save considerable operating costs by not using the railway. By the end of 1975 it was clear that the case for reopening had been lost. Being a light railway there were few substantial engineering or earthworks, although the land taken for Lambourn station was considerable. Little trace now remains of the line.

Far top left: On Saturday 3 November 1973 the WR ran four special trains to mark the end of freight services over the Newbury to Welford Park section of the Lambourn branch. The trains were formed by a nine car DMU. The second of these, the 11.40am from Newbury, is seen here arriving at Welford Park. *G. F. Gillham*

Far top right: The LCGB special at Speen on 14 February 1970. *D. E. Canning*

Left: LCGB special approaches Boxford *en route* to Welford also on 14 February 1970. *D. E. Canning*

Above: The abandoned Lambourn branch, south of Lambourn, crossed one of the roads leading into the town on the level. In June 1993 the track bed had been reclaimed for agricultural use, but gate posts and fencing remained. *Author*

Below: Lambourn station in June 1993. Very little of the original station remains. *Author*

⑥ Lost links with Oxford

The ancient university centre of Oxford resisted being connected to the railways, but in 1844 the first line reached the edge of the city. Two decades later a network of branches ran to the city or had connections to it. The main lines in the area had been conceived with, above all, speed and directness in mind and accordingly bypassed some significant towns. As a consequence, a number of short connecting branch lines existed.

All Change at Radley

Abingdon shared Oxford's dislike for the railway and rejected a line proposed to the riverside town in 1837. It was not until June 1856 that the Abingdon Railway's 2-mile broad gauge line reached the town. It was modified to standard gauge in 1872 and subsequently extended almost 1 mile along the Oxford to Didcot line to a junction at Radley. From 1860 it was operated by the Great Western Railway until nationalisation. It was closed to passenger traffic in September 1963, although freight remained to the Abingdon maltings for some time after. Radley station remains open and the former GWR junction sign is preserved at the Great Western Society's Didcot Railway Centre. The line had few engineering works, but it can still be

Above: Radley junction and signalbox signs have been preserved at the Didcot Railway Centre. Author

Below: Radley, the junction for Abingdon, became an unstaffed halt in March 1967. Demolition of the station had started when this photograph was taken in April 1967. Looking towards Oxford, the Abingdon platform is on the far left of the picture. A. Muckley

Right: Class 33 No 6550 passes Radley with a Fawley to Northampton oil train on 23 July 1973. By this time Radley station buildings had been completely demolished. Looking towards Didcot, Abingdon trains departed from the platform on the right. *G. F. Bannister*

Below: The convenient road interchange at Abingdon station. A single unit railcar waits in the station in the 1960s. Abingdon-built MG cars once provided freight on this branch. *Ian Allan Library*

traced for much of its route, although Abingdon station has been redeveloped.

1066 And All That

The Wallingford and Watlington Railway was a standard gauge branch off the GWR's London to Bristol line at Cholsey and Moulsford. William the Conqueror had crossed the River Thames at Wallingford in 1066. Eight hundred years later in July 1866 when the railway line opened, it failed in its attempt to cross the Thames here, so it never reached its intended target of Watlington. The 2¾-mile line was worked by the

Right: The Thames Valley Rambler three-car DMU at Abingdon on 29 October 1977. By this time the station buildings had been demolished. By the early 1990s there was little or no trace of any rail activity on this site.
R. Tomkins

Below: 'All Change'. 0-4-2T (Tank engine) No 1466 (not 1066!) enters Cholsey and Moulsford station during the GW Society's open day on the Wallingford branch on 15 April 1968.
C. J. Mills

GWR from its opening. It closed to passengers in June 1959 and the original terminus to goods in 1965 when the line was cut back to an industrial area in Wallingford. Freight on this section ended in June 1981.

Unlike many other Oxfordshire branches this was not the end of the story. The track is *in situ* from Cholsey station, which remains open, to a new platform at Wallingford located some way short of the old terminus, which has now been redeveloped as a housing area. The line is run by the Cholsey and Wallingford Railway.

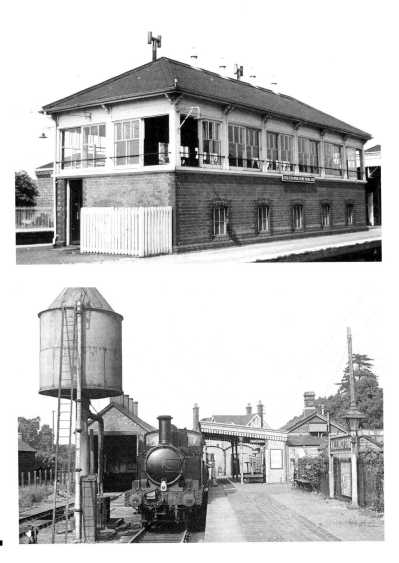

The Secret Garden

The 3¾ mile line to the ancient town of Woodstock, as with the Abingdon line, was extended to a convenient main line station and ran for about a mile alongside the main Oxford to Worcester line from Kidlington, before turning westward to reach an attractive stone terminus on the edge of Woodstock. The Woodstock Railway was funded by the Duke of Marlborough, whose gates to Blenheim Palace were virtually opposite the station. For a time the station was even named after his palatial home and called Blenheim and Woodstock. The line opened in May 1890 and was worked by the GWR, chiefly with auto-trains of one or two coaches. The branch line had one intermediate halt, Shipton-on-Cherwell. Although some trains ran to Oxford, they could not compete

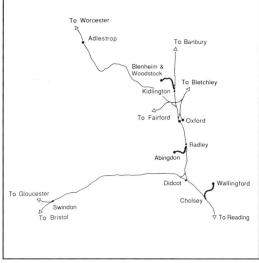

with the more direct buses and the line was an early candidate for closure. The last train ran in March 1954 and Kidlington station closed a decade later. Whilst little remains of the line itself, the terminal station is in use as a garage. Behind the garage is a secret garden; the station gardens with their topiary hedges are almost the same today as when the last train pulled out.

Above left: Wallingford station, September 1967. Author

Below: Wallingford station area, July 1990. Orientate yourself with the tall chimney. Author

Above: Kidlington station on 5 August 1950. Saint Class 4-6-0 No 2981 Ivanhoe heads the 3.50 pm Oxford to Leamington train whilst 0-4-2T No 1450 heads the 4.10 pm to Woodstock. W. A. Camwell

Right: Gas lamp-posts and the station gardens remain hidden behind the garage at Woodstock in June 1993. Author

Below: Woodstock station in June 1993 and in use as a garage. Author

7 Adlestrop

Closures of individual stations were not limited to branch lines; a mass of closures have occurred on main lines that remain open. In some cases the station's demise resulted from a line being unable to provide the capacity for both main line and stopping services. However, this was not usually the case; many small stations on main lines were built for operating purposes, or more usually simply opportunistically, because there was a settlement nearby.

One such station to close in June 1966 was Adlestrop, on the Oxford to Worcester line. The station was located some considerable distance from the small village of that name, a fact which expedited its downfall. The station may have closed, but one of the

station's name boards remains preserved in the village. Under the name is a GWR seat with a poem inscribed on it. For it was here that Edward Thomas (1878-1917) produced his evocative poem *Adlestrop* that recalls his passion for the English countryside and implies that even before World War I few passengers were using the station:

'Yes, I remember Adlestrop –
The name, because one afternoon
Of heat the express-train drew up there
Unwontedly. It was late June.

The steam hissed. Someone cleared his throat.
No one left and no one came
On the bare platform. What I saw
Was Adlestrop – only the name

And willows, willow-herb, and grass,
And meadowsweet, and haycocks dry,
No whit less still and lonely fair
Than the high cloudlets in the sky.

And for that minute a blackbird sang
Close by, and round him, mistier,
Farther and farther, all the birds
Of Oxfordshire and Gloucestershire.'

Sadly, Thomas was killed in action in World War I. The station is closed. Yet somehow this is not the end of the story. Such is the atmosphere created by the poem that the station, which still retains some buildings, lives on, together with the beautiful and unspoilt surrounding Cotswold Hills.

Above left: The village shelter at Adlestrop containing the station sign and station seat, in June 1993. Author

Left: The site of Adlestrop station on the Oxford to Worcester line, June 1993. Author

Above: The entrance to Adlestrop station, June 1993. Author

⑧ Swindon's mighty works

To continue for a moment with a poetry theme, I am reminded of:

' *"My name is Ozymandias, king of kings:*
Look on my works, ye mighty, and despair!"
Nothing beside remains...'

This quotation from Shelley's poem, essentially about how the mighty have fallen, is not without some poignancy to Swindon. The railway works in the town, which had carriage, wagon and locomotive shops, became the centre of the GWR empire and arguably the greatest railway works of all time.

SWINDON WORKS HOOTER				
MONDAY to THURSDAY		FRIDAY		
TIME	DURATION	TIME	DURATION	
6·45	17 SECS	6·45	17 SECS	
7·20	12 SECS	7·20	12 SECS	
7·25	7 SECS	7·25	7 SECS	
7·30	12 SECS	7·30	12 SECS	
12·30	12 SECS	1·30	12 SECS	
1:05	12 SECS			
1·10	7 SECS			
1·15	12 SECS			
4·30	12 SECS			

Left: Swindon works hooter table in August 1982; ideal if you wanted wakening at 6.45! *C. G. Maggs*

Below: 'A' Shop at Swindon works in full operation in July 1962. *J. W. Rainey*

Right: This aerial view of Swindon in its heyday gives some idea of the scale of the works area. *Aerofilms Ltd*

Below right: Hooters, which still survive, above the hooter house at Swindon works, August 1982. *C. G. Maggs*

In the 1840s the town had a population of about 2,500. The astonishing success of the GWR demanded the provision of a new and central works to serve the rapidly developing railway. Swindon was at the junction of the Cheltenham branch and also at a useful engine working division on the line from Paddington to Bristol. Construction of the works started in 1841 and much of the stone used was that extracted from Box Tunnel. By 1843 the works were in operation and over 400 were employed. As the railway prospered, so the works developed. It started constructing engines and from 1861 manufactured its own rails. Later Swindon was selected as the site for the carriage and wagon works. Even more buildings were added and the first coaches built at Swindon entered service in 1869.

By 1900 the population of Swindon had risen to over 45,000. In order to accommodate the ever increasing workforce, a new village of eight streets had been constructed. Educational, medical, recreational and religious requirements were all taken into account. The new village was situated very conveniently for the works and a series of alleyways led to one of the main entrances, which in turn provided a long subway under the main line to reach the works. In addition to family housing, a barracks was provided for unmarried men, but this was not popular and was

Right: Although many buildings have been demolished at Swindon works a number still remain, in varying condition, including these photographed in June 1993. *Author*

Below: The tunnel entrance to Swindon works. The scale of buildings remaining at Swindon works can be ascertained from this photograph taken in June 1993. *Author*

Far right: Map of Swindon 1889. Compare with map on page 36 dated 1901 and that on page 37 dated 1942. *Crown Copyright*

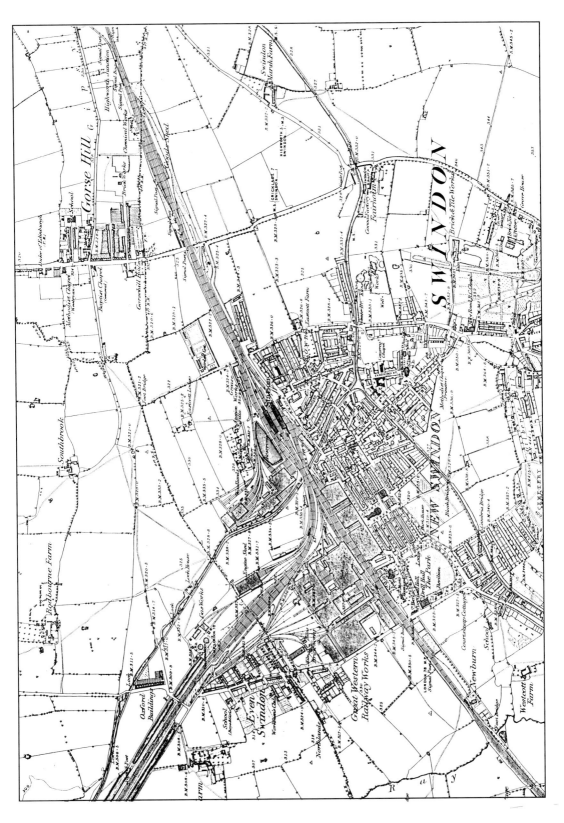

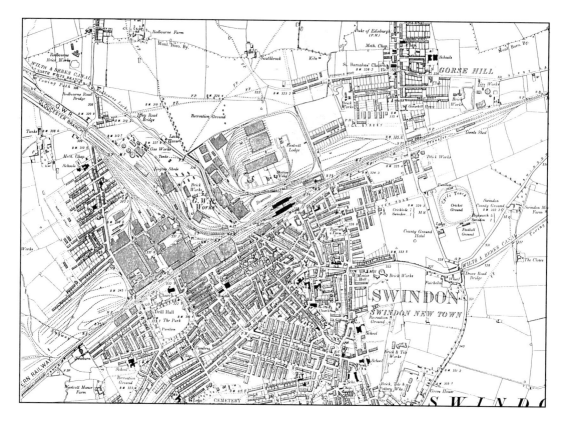

converted into a chapel. Later it became a shrine to the GWR when in 1963 it became a railway museum.

As the size of engines increased and as the railway grew, so did the size of the works at Swindon. In one year alone the dimensions of the engine shed were doubled. Water was piped in from Kemble and in 1907 the gas works was extended to become the largest in Europe, although savings were made in the village when gas lights were not lit during the week of a full moon! By the 1920s the works area had utilized most of the available land, covering over 300 acres and employing about 14,000 people. Even after nationalisation some additions were made and by 1959 about 85 acres of the works area were roofed and a mass of lines served the works.

Then came the era of standardisation of steam locomotives and dieselisation. A gradual decline set in. In the 1960s many of the old buildings were demolished and the carriage and wagon side ended. The already diminished workforce was reduced by a further 3,000 down to 5,000 and the last steam locomotive built for BR, *Evening Star*, was completed at the works. The withdrawal of the Western Region's distinctive diesel hydraulic fleet resulted in further reductions and by 1975 the works were using only about half the available site area and only about 34 acres were roofed.

The works underwent further rationalisation and contraction and some of the buildings were sold off; but their future looked assured and it was felt that the link between the town and works would have a long and distinguished future. 1985 saw the 150th anniversary of the formation of the GWR; this was to be a time of celebration. The works still employed about 1,500. It therefore came as a great shock when it was announced that the works were to close the following year. Most of the vast area of lines associated with the works have since been removed, but a number of the substantial and distinctive buildings associated with the site remain and some even continue in railway use. Indeed in 1990 part of the site was used to display items from the National Railway Museum while the roof at the York museum was being repaired, the main offices are now reused and there are long-term plans to turn the area into a thriving new community.

Above right: The CME's building on 2 June 1982. The carvings of a 'Fire Fly' class engine came from the original engine shed opened on 1 January 1843. *C. G. Maggs*

Above far right: The GWR's model village at Swindon was very advanced for its time and the architecture has stood the test of time. The village is still fully occupied today. All alleyways such as the one shown here in 1993, led to the tunnel entrance of Swindon works. *Author*

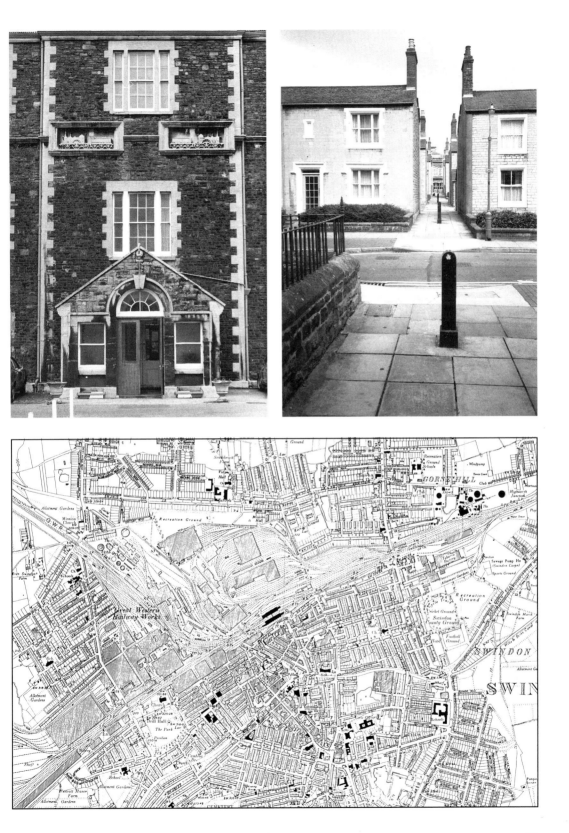

⑨ Cirencester: connections and change

The Roman roads of the Icknield Way and Ermine Street connected with the Fosse Way at the Roman community named Corinium, now better known as Cirencester. In more recent times this attractive market town, which serves a considerable part of the Cotswolds, was also the focus of railway activity, both actual and proposed. The first line to the town ran from Swindon directly to Cirencester, being completed in May 1841. However, in 1845 the Cirencester section became the end of a 4½-mile branch from Kemble when a second line was built running north-west from Kemble towards Cheltenham.

This was not the end of the story as far as Cirencester was concerned. The Midland and South

Right: Cirencester Town in June 1993. Author

Below: 0-6-0PT No 3739 on a passenger train at Cirencester Town station in the 1950s. D. Lawrence

Western Junction Railway (M&SWJR), deemed a trespasser by the GWR, opened its 15-mile line from Rushey Platt at Swindon to Cirencester in December 1883, thus providing Cirencester with another route south. The M&SWJR line was extended some 13 miles north to Andoversford Junction in 1891 to link Cirencester directly to Cheltenham, whilst the company established its own mini 'Swindon' works at Cirencester.

Other proposals for railway routes were also considered to connect with the existing lines at Cirencester. Fairford was the isolated terminal of a GWR rural branch line from Oxford. The line had been opened in 1861, as far as Fairford, but the original

39

Left: The simply constructed Chesterton Lane Halt in the summer of 1963 looking from Kemble. A. Muckley

Bottom left: Kemble station in the early 1960s. P. J. Sharpe

Right: Kemble station in September 1969 looking towards Cirencester. The platform canopy has been removed and the siding was sometimes used to store track machines. Author

Below: 0-6-0PT No 7411 at Fairford with the 9.6 am to Oxford on 6 August 1950. W. A. Camwell

intention was to continue on to Cirencester. The scheme was again contemplated in the 1930s, but although Fairford station was designed as an intermediate station, with the line tantalizingly extending westward, it remained the end of the line until its closure in June 1962. The M&SWJR also had plans to link Cirencester to Berkeley Road via Nailsworth, but this proposal came to nothing and the opportunity of

Left: Kemble station in 1984. This most attractive station was once a junction for both Tetbury and Cirencester. The line shown is that to Cirencester, although it ran only just beyond the station platform. Author

Bottom left: Fairford signalbox in August 1969. Author

Bottom right: Fairford station in August 1969. At this time Concorde was being tested at the nearby Fairford airfield. Author

Top: Fairford station in August 1988. This certainly shows the buildings in a better condition; the station was being used as a road transport depot. Author

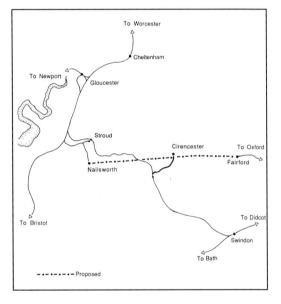

changing trains to travel onwards east and west at Cirencester was lost.

The old M&SWJR line was the first to close, in September 1961. In contrast, the former GWR Cirencester Town station was both relatively well used and well sited. It was consequently believed that the introduction of lightweight four-wheeled diesel railcars and additional halts on the line might just save this branch. They did actually attract more passengers, but not in adequate numbers, and the branch closed in April 1964. Freight lingered on a little longer until October 1965.

The stone station building at Cirencester is both attractive and intriguing. It is a listed building. Permission to demolish the station was refused and the building is in use as offices and as public conveniences. Today it is located in a sea of cars, the former station yard having been turned into a town centre car park.

10 A bridge too far

For some years the GWR was nicknamed the 'Great Way Round', mainly because the route from London to South Wales involved a detour around the Severn Estuary via Gloucester. As a consequence several designs were advanced over the years for the erection of a bridge over the Severn. Amongst the initial suggestions there was even one with the foresight to provide for road traffic as well as the railway. However, the final outcome was the opening by the Severn Bridge Railway Company in 1879 of the long

Left: Severn Bridge for Blakeney Halt with the Severn Bridge in the background on the former Berkeley Road to Lydney Town branch line. This photograph was taken from the 1.10 pm ex-Lydney Town auto-train. R. E. Toop.

Below: The Severn Bridge showing the ten masonry arches at the Lydney side, with the breach caused by the accident of 1960. S. T. Allen

and impressive Severn Bridge. The bridge had twenty-one spans of bow string girders on metal cylindrical columns of which two spans were 327ft long. It provided a headway of 70ft above high water level and had a total length of 4,162ft. The Gloucester and Sharpness Canal was crossed by a 400-ton swing bridge which was operated by a steam engine and supported on a substantial stone tower built under the centre of the swing section.

The Severn Bridge reduced the journey between London and South Wales by about 30 miles, but the opening of the Severn Tunnel to passengers in 1886 saw a decline in the use of the bridge which involved a longer journey to South Wales than via the tunnel. As a consequence the operating company soon found itself in a financial crisis and in 1894 the bridge was acquired by the Great Western and Midland Railways. They formed the Severn and Wye Joint Railway which ran the line over the bridge, together with lines into the Forest of Dean. The bridge was a useful diversionary route when the Severn Tunnel was under repair, but traffic continued to decline and passenger services were limited to a few local services between Lydney and Berkeley Road.

Closure of the bridge came in an unexpected and calamitous fashion. On the foggy evening of 25 October 1960 the bridge was hit by a 299-ton petrol tanker named Wastdale. One of the piers, simultaneously with two spans of the bridge, was demolished. Five lives were lost that night in the Severn, but casualties could have been higher as the accident happened just after a train had crossed the bridge.

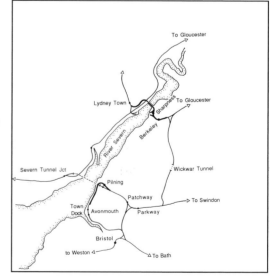

Above: The circular tower that housed part of the turning mechanism for the swing section of the Severn Bridge, looking like a Martello tower in June 1993. *Author*

Above right: Although the Severn Bridge has gone, a reminder of the general design of the bridge can be found in Sharpness docks. This view shows the swing section in June 1993, but alas a railway no longer runs over this bridge. *Author*

It was decided not to restore the bridge and for a time passenger services ran only from Berkeley Road to Sharpness, but this service was withdrawn in November 1964. The bridge was demolished by 1970, but a reminder of the scale of the structure can be gained from the circular tower that supported the swing section of the bridge over the Gloucester and Sharpness Canal. A smaller version of this section of the bridge still exists at Sharpness docks, although ironically the rail track has been replaced by a road.

Right: Map of the Severn Bridge 1924. *Crown Copyright*

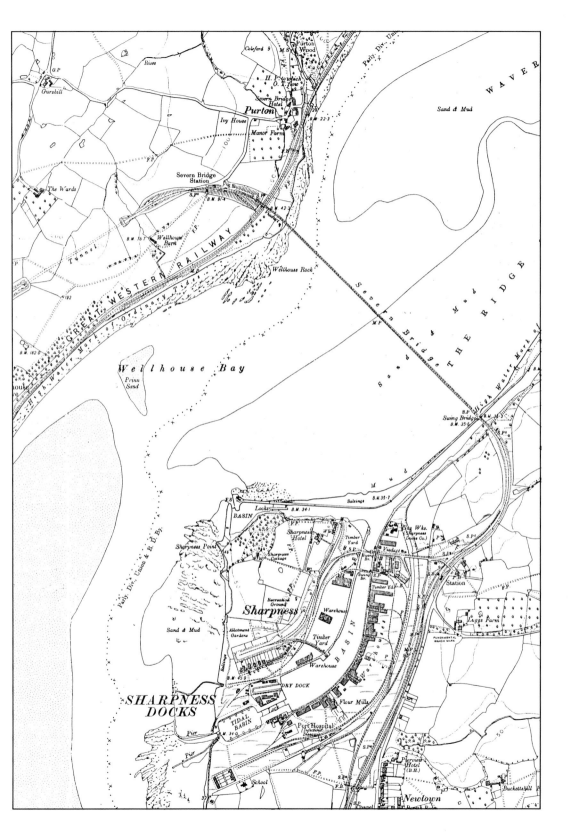

49

11 The Severn Valley Railway

The Severn Valley Railway travels through a unique area, the lush and attractive countryside belying the fact that in earlier times the banks of the River Severn in these parts were a great hive of industry. The area was once a principal iron working district in Britain; indeed the first iron rails were made at Coalbrookdale. Yet even as the railways arrived, so the supply of raw materials had been largely exhausted and the affluence of the area declined.

The original Severn Valley Railway opened, as a subsidiary of the Oxford, Worcester and

Right: The tracks remain tantalizingly in position at Iron Bridge station. This is a view looking to the Iron Bridge in June 1993. Author

Below: Stourport-on-Severn on 3 January 1970, the last day of services over this section of the line. The 12.55 pm Saturdays only train from Kidderminster waits at the station. J. G. Glover

Far right: Public Notice of Withdrawal of Passenger Services on the Severn Valley line from 9 September 1963. A. Muckley

BRITISH RAILWAYS BOARD

LONDON MIDLAND REGION

PUBLIC NOTICE

With the consent of the Ministry of Transport, the British Railways Board hereby give notice that on and from Monday, 9th September, 1963, the passenger train service between SHREWSBURY AND BEWDLEY will be discontinued; BERRINGTON, CRESSAGE, BUILDWAS, IRONBRIDGE & BROSE-LEY, COALPORT, BRIDGNORTH, HAMPTON LOADE, HIGHLEY, ARLEY STATIONS, COUND, JACKFIELD, LINLEY, EARDINGTON, °ALVELEY, AND NORTHWOOD HALTS will be closed to passengers.

°-N.C.B. Private Halt

The passenger train services between BEWDLEY AND KIDDERMINSTER and between BEWDLEY AND HARTLEBURY will be reduced.

Alternative passenger road services are already operated in the area by the following operators, from whom details of omnibus services may be obtained:-

Birmingham & Midland Motor Omnibus Company Ltd.
Wolverhampton Corporation Transport.
J. T. Whittle & Son, Highley.

Any further information required in respect of these arrangements can be obtained upon application to:-

Mr. E. R. WILLIAMS,
Divisional Manager,
London Midland Region,
43, Smallbrook, Ringway,
BIRMINGHAM, 5.
Telephone: Birmingham MIDland 5050 Ext. 303.

or Station Masters at:-

SHREWSBURY	Tel: Shrewsbury 3614
BERRINGTON	–
CRESSAGE	Tel: Cressage 312
BUILDWAS	Tel: Ironbridge 2185
IRONBRIDGE & BROSELEY	Tel: Ironbridge 2118
BRIDGNORTH	Tel: Bridgnorth 2208
HAMPTON LOADE	Tel: Quatt 221
HIGHLEY	Tel: Bridgnorth 2208
ARLEY	Tel: Bewdley 2242
BEWDLEY	Tel: Bewdley 2242
STOURPORT-ON-SEVERN	Tel: Stourport 2331
HARTLEBURY	Tel: Hartlebury 231
KIDDERMINSTER	Tel: Kidderminster 4004

BR. 35014   D-185 P.   July 1963

PRINTED BY JOSEPH WONES LTD. OF WEST BROMWICH AND WEDNESBURY

Wolverhampton Railway, in February 1862. Linking Hartlebury with Shrewsbury via Bewdley, Bridgnorth, Coalport and Iron Bridge it provided a 39½-mile direct route between Shrewsbury and Worcester. As its name suggests, it ran along and crossed the upper reaches of the River Severn. It became part of the Great Western Railway, who in June 1878 opened a 3½-mile line to connect Bewdley with Kidderminster. Other connections included a link to Wyre Forest, whilst those to Wellington, Shifnal, and Craven Arms could be made at Buildwas.

It was perhaps somewhat indicative of the gradual decline of the line that this former GWR route was included in, and proposed for closure by, the London Midland Region. The line was closed to passengers in September 1963 and for freight to the Alveley coal area south of Bridgnorth in 1969. The service from Bewdley to Kidderminster and Hartlebury ran until January 1970.

This, however, was not the end of the story. In 1965 a group of enthusiasts established the Severn Valley Railway (SVR). Today it is one of the foremost preservation organisations. It has since restored the line, through some of the most beautiful scenery

Above: Linley Halt with a Bewdley to Shrewsbury railcar. A. Muckley

Left: Coalport station in September 1993. Author

Above; Shrewsbury to Hartlebury railcar pauses at Coalport on 24 August 1963. A. Muckley

Left: Between Iron Bridge and Buildwas the line is overgrown but is used as a footpath. R. Trill

along the River Severn, to Bridgnorth from Kidderminster via Bewdley. The Severn Valley Railway has about 16 route miles and the UK's largest working collection of preserved locomotives, together with coaches and goods wagons from many different railway companies, but the line itself has a distinctly GWR secondary route atmosphere.

The 22 miles northwards beyond Bridgnorth to Shrewsbury has been lost, probably for ever. There are stability problems, and both housing and a golf course block the line near Bridgnorth. Whilst this is unfortunate, as the route runs through Iron Bridge which in many ways was the birthplace of the Industrial Revolution, a most attractive and interesting section of line has been saved. Part of the closed route around Coalport and Iron Bridge is used as a footpath. In 1994 BR rails still link in to the power station near Buildwas from the Shrewsbury to Birmingham line. The SVR guide suggests that the line is unlikely to be extended further. I speculate that one day passengers will again cross the bridge at Iron Bridge to catch a Severn Valley Railway train!

Left: BR Standard Class 4 tank No 80100, which was transferred from the London, Tilbury & Southend line, brings the 11.35am Bridgnorth to Shrewsbury service into Iron Bridge. Ian Allan Library

Below left: Connecting trains, but few passengers at Buildwas station in the 1950s. Real Photographs Co

Right: Arley station looking south towards Bewdley in May 1972. A. Muckley

Above: Part of the route beyond Iron Bridge hugs the narrow Severn Gorge by means of a viaduct and retaining wall. R. Trill

Left: A number of accessories have been added at Arley after the line was reopened by the Severn Valley Railway as this view taken in August 1992 shows. Author

Above: Manor meets *Manor*. No 7819 *Hinton Manor* runs round its train while No 7812 *Erlestoke Manor* awaits the 'road' at Bewdley on 1 September 1979. *P. Skelton*

Above left: Foley Park, a typical GWR halt opened in 1905, between Kidderminster and Bewdley in March 1966. *A. Muckley*

Left: The same view looking west and showing the typical GWR 'pagoda style' waiting room in January 1976, today nothing remains of the halt. *A. Muckley*

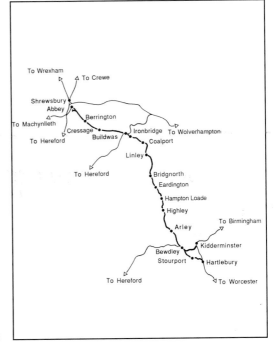

12 Birmingham: a tale of two stations

Birmingham, as Britain's second largest city, saw its greatest expansion during the Industrial Revolution. At its industrial zenith, the sky glowed red at night from blast furnaces and it was said to manufacture everything from a pin to a cannon. Its development continued in Victorian times, aided and abetted by the railways. Birmingham is unusual in that it was not established on the site of a river, or at an early road crossing, but was in fact located on a hill which meant that tunnels, cuttings and some heavy gradients were required to reach its central stations. Considerable if gradual change took place between the World Wars when older industries dwindled together with Birmingham's population. The decline, like its growth, was mirrored in Birmingham's railways.

Snow Hill

A temporary station was provided in 1852 at the terminus of the GWR's broad gauge line from London and first assumed the name of Snow Hill in 1858. As with some other GWR temporary stations, it continued in use for some time before it was displaced by a more lasting building in 1871. As Birmingham developed, increased commuting, coupled with increased train services on the line through Snow Hill, which had been extended to Wolverhampton and the North West, meant that the station became increasingly congested.

In addition, as a competitor to the London and North Western Railway, the GWR became increasingly anxious at the failings of its main Birmingham

Below: Platform 12 was normally used by Stourbridge local services, but on 11 June 1963 it was used by this mixed service hauled by 4-6-0 No 5093 Upton Castle. The amount of glass behind the engine led to Snow Hill being known as the Crystal Palace of the GWR. *B. J. Ashworth*

Right: 2-6-2T No 5101 has arrived at Snow Hill with the 4.35 pm from Stourbridge Junction via Dudley on 30 August 1958. *M. Mensing*

Bottom right: NRM Poster. There was fierce competition between the LNWR and GWR for London and Birmingham passengers

Left : Snow Hill was damaged in an air raid in November 1940 as this view of the restaurant, which appears to be used as a dormitory, shows. British Railways

Below: 4-6-0 No 5992 Horton Hall passes Snow Hill with a down freight on 24 October 1964. The station has suffered a remarkable deterioration compared with the photograph taken in 1958.
J. H. Cooper-Smith

station. Consequently in 1906 the construction of a greatly improved and enlarged Snow Hill station was started. The new station was roughly twice as spacious as the old and basically incorporated two enormous island platforms over 1,000ft in length. The central feature of the station was the huge roof which was of ridge and furrow design. It was over 500ft long and virtually 6,000 tons of iron and steel were employed in its assembly. By 1912 the new station was largely complete and, because of the amount of glass used in the roof and side walls, became known as the Crystal Palace of the GWR.

The station operated without significant change until its closure, although it was damaged by enemy action in World War 2 which also effectively put an end to plans for a new hotel frontage. In any event expansion on the site was difficult as the eastern approaches were restricted by a tunnel. The tunnel

contained a clapperboard which banged against the side of trains to inform drivers, in the often smoke-filled hole, that they were approaching Snow Hill station.

In 1954 suburban services were put on regular interval timings, in 1960 a new power box was opened and it looked as if this substantial and well established station would have a long and assured future.

This was not to be; three years later the Western Region's lines through Snow Hill were taken over by the London Midland Region. Once electrification extended to Birmingham's New Street station, Snow Hill's destiny was sealed. Whilst a 105min schedule had been devised as far back as 1938 for the London trains, the LMR schedules for the former GWR line were slowed to 115min.

Above: All is not what it appears. Seemingly a classic study of an express at Snow Hill, closer inspection will reveal no locomotive and a DMU. This is the 5.40 pm departure for Hereford and Cardiff on 12 June 1958. It is formed of a six-car DMU with an extra coach attached to give additional accommodation.
M. Mensing

*Right: S*now Hill's last Saturday, 4 March 1967, as a main line. Six soccer specials, plus two Ian Allan Last Steam Specials augmented the usual service. Meanwhile, in a quieter moment that day, a Brush Type 4 passes with a freight on the 'down' through road. *J. H. Cooper-Smith*

ELEVATION TO COLMORE ROW

By 1968 the main line services had been diverted to other routes and the station was all but closed. However, two local services continued, including those to Wolverhampton Low Level, this once congested main line being reduced in its final days to an infrequent single carriage. Although a battle was mounted to rescue the station, its remaining services closed in March 1972. For a number of years the station site remained in the city centre in an ever worse derelict state until the vast train shed was demolished in 1977.

Yet this was not the end of the story. The site was redeveloped and included a new, albeit smaller, Snow Hill station which opened in October 1987. Against all

G.W.R.

Birmingham

(SNOW HILL)

Above: Plans were revealed in 1939 for a new Great Western Hotel to replace the existing frontage at Snow Hill station. The outbreak of World War 2 put an end to this plan. *British Railways*

Right: The eight ticket booths on the concourse were not in heavy demand in the week before closure as this photograph taken on 1 March 1967 shows. *A. Muckley*

the odds, by 1993 through trains ran once again from
Snow Hill to London. By 1995 track should extend
back to Smethwick to provide a second cross-city line
and will one day return to Wolverhampton, whose
former GWR buildings still remain.

Moor Street

The GWR worked the Birmingham and Henley-in-
Arden Railway from its commencement and the terminus of the line was constructed at Birmingham
Moor Street. This was built in classic Great Western
style and was opened in June 1894, chiefly for
Birmingham's expanding suburban services. It was
agreeable, almost like a small seaside town terminus

Right: Moor Street on 30 July 1981 with Saturday shoppers arriving. The cut away part of the platform was for the former traverser used in steam days to switch engines from one track to another. J. G. Glover

Below: Two police officers stand guarding No 7029 Clun Castle at Snow Hill, ready for HRH Prince Charles on 14 September 1988. This was the first steam service to return to the station after its reopening in 1987. S. Widdowson.

Left: Moor Street station in festive mood on 25 September 1987, yet on its penultimate day of regular operation. Author

Below: A DMU awaits departure at Moor Street station on 25 September 1987. The new station can be seen on the far right. Author

in scale, altogether of different proportions from Snow Hill. Moor Street usually operated efficiently and was generally appreciated by the passengers it served.

The passenger station survived right until September 1987, whilst subsequently demolition has been resisted. A new, much smaller station has been built alongside the old GWR station, retaining the Moor Street name and serving many of its former routes. There are hopes that much of Moor Street can be retained in any redevelopment of the area and that the station may be used as a terminal for steam activities associated with the Birmingham Railway Museum at Tyseley.

Above left: Moor Street signalbox, GW signals and platform end in July 1966. Author

Above: Moor Street unused, but remaining in reasonable condition, September 1993. R. Trill.

Below: Moor Street unused, overgrown and derelict in September 1993 awaits the return of trains. R. Trill

13 A souvenir of the Somerset and Dorset

The medicinal waters of Bath have been exploited since Roman times, but in the eighteenth century John Wood undertook remarkable town planning in the city. This was accomplished so adeptly that Bath became the most stylish locality in Britain. As a result when the railways arrived, stations, bridges and viaducts were built very attractively to ensure as much harmony with the existing buildings as possible.

This was undoubtedly the situation with Green Park station. The architect was J. H. Sanders and the station's classical stone exterior with its magnificent Ionic columns, balustered parapet and grand windows, combined with the straightforward train shed, is exceptionally appealing. Although the station was

built for the Midland Railway (MR) in 1870, as the terminal of its line from Mangotsfield, it was later used by the Somerset and Dorset Railway (S&DR). It is the connection with this fascinating railway for which the station is well remembered and as from 1958 onwards it ended its days in the WR, I have included it in this volume.

The S&DR opened its 26-mile line from Evercreech Junction over the Mendip Hills and via Radstock, Wellow and Midford into the station in July 1874. The cost of construction entirely depleted the assets of the S&DR and financial difficulties compelled the company to turn to the MR and L&SWR for help. They consented to take over the railway, but continued to use the S&DR title until nationalisation.

Left: The classical frontage of Bath Green Park station in May 1964. With the exception of the significant growth of a tree, the frontage remains largely unchanged 30 years later. *M. C. Burdge*

Below: '8F' No 48760 is pictured at Bath Green Park with the stock for the 8.15am to Templecombe on 5 March 1966. *Derek Cross*

Before 1951 the station was in fact known as Queen Square. The change in name to Green Park was a prelude to other changes as the former S&DR line became a pawn in regional boundary adjustments. Such a state of affairs was not good news and after a number of postponements, involving a final two month reprieve when a very limited service operated over the former S&DR line, all remaining services to the station were withdrawn and the station was closed in March 1966.

The station remained unused and deteriorating amid proposals for its demolition until 1979, when there were plans to convert the site into a super-market. The classical frontage was described at the subsequent planning inquiry as probably the best Victorian building in the City of Bath and its destruction was prevented. Certainly now that it has been restored to its former glory, in connection with the supermarket development, the station looks as splendid as ever.

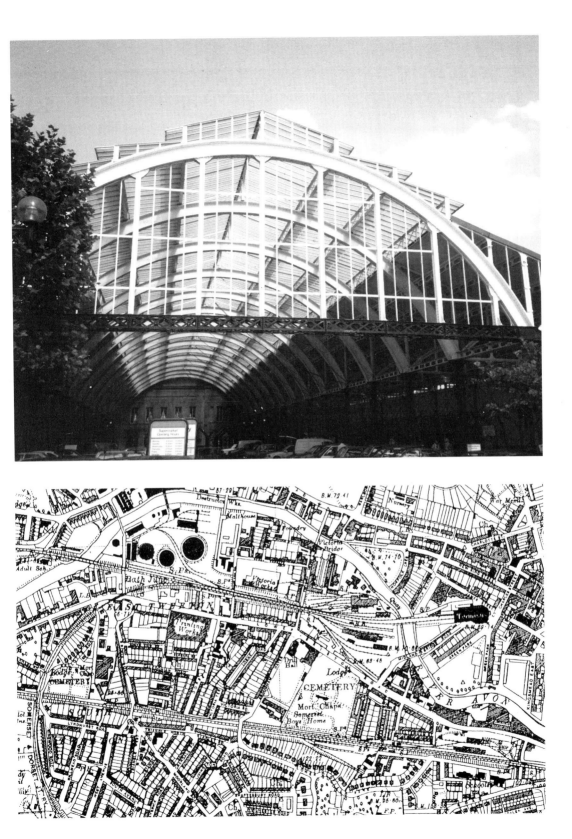

Bristol has prominent associations with Brunel. His first station at Temple Meads in the city was on part of the 'meads' in the parish of 'Temple', but it was a temple in its own right at the very start of the broad gauge Great Western Railway. The stone building was effectively divided into three sections: an office block, an engine shed and the awe-inspiring train shed consisting of two platforms, separated by sidings and covered by a 72ft wide wood and iron hammer-beam styled roof, which was some 220ft long. Completed in 1841, it is one of the most celebrated monuments to the birth of the railways.

Left: The engine shed at the very end of Brunel's station and the GWR's line at Bristol Temple Meads in August 1980. C. G. Maggs

Below: Brunel's Temple Meads station in use as a car park in 1969. British Railways

Right: A view of Brunel's original train shed, the later addition in the foreground and the engine shed in the far distance in October 1965. C. G. Maggs

Far right: The original Brunel train shed with its hammer-beam roof has happily been restored and in 1993 remained in good condition. R. Trill

Below right: The original Brunel train shed, now a function centre, has been separated from the later addition which in 1993 was used as a car park. Author

Shortly after Brunel's station was opened, the Bristol and Exeter Railway ran a line at right angles to the building and, although it had its own terminus, a curve was constructed to enable its trains to use the GWR station. Furthermore, the Bristol and Gloucester Railway from 1844 also ran to the station and congestion ensued. As a plan to extend the railways into a new station at Queen Square was rebuffed by the City Council, the railway companies decided to build a new joint station at Temple Meads. This was considerably reconstructed between 1865 and 1878, when a new train shed was affixed to Brunel's. The station operated with little change until it was again extended in the 1930s. Brunel's original station building was retained in all the changes, but it gradually fell out of use with only one or two trains departing from the old platform 15. From 1965 it was used as a car park. There was great concern that such an important historic building was falling into disrepair and in the 1980s it was restored to much of its original splendour and put to recreational uses.

From Bristol Temple Meads an interesting railway still runs via Clifton and Avonmouth Dock to Severn Beach. Originally the branch line continued on to Pilning Low Level, which enabled trains to run back to Temple Meads via a circular route by joining the main line between the Severn Tunnel and Bristol at Pilning South Wales Junction.

The first section of the line towards Severn Beach reached Clifton Down in 1874 and then via the Clifton Tunnel to Avonmouth in 1877, although passenger services did not commence on this section until 1885, almost a decade after its opening. The 7¾-mile Avonmouth to Pilning line was opened to freight in

Left: Did Brunel, like his railway, invent immortality? This sign was noted at Bristol station in 1993. R. Trill

Below: The spartan New Passage Halt before its closure. C. G. Maggs

Right: Severn Beach station, September 1993. The current end of the line. R. Trill

Right below: Cross Hands Halt. C. G. Maggs

February 1900. This section broadly followed the Severn Estuary, crossing over the Severn Tunnel before reaching the small settlement of New Passage. This was the terminus of an old route to the stone pier which once provided a Severn ferry crossing to Portskewett, but which went out of business with the opening of the Severn Tunnel. Again it was some time before passenger services were inaugurated over the freight route, but in June 1928 trains to Avonmouth were extended to Severn Beach and to a number of fairly spartan halts on the line, including the low level halt at Pilning which was situated beside the high level halt on the main line. The line from Severn Beach to Pilning was closed to passengers in November 1964 and to all traffic in July 1968. The section from Bristol to Severn Beach survived the cuts.

My diary reports a trip on this line:

21 JULY 1969; Severn Beach is a resort past its best and the general air of dereliction is portrayed in the station. The journey to Bristol is quite diverse, firstly following the sea then a mass of lines at Avonmouth before a view of the Avon Gorge appears. Finally, you trundle through Victorian suburbs to Bristol TM.

Little has changed since that was written. A section of the closed trackbed north of Severn Beach has been used by lorries involved in the construction of the second Severn road bridge.

Above: Pilning Low Level Halt. *C. G. Maggs*

Left: The track in the foreground leading to Pilning at Severn Beach station, 21 July 1969. *Author*

Below: The remains of the the stone New Passage Pier which fell out of use once the Severn Tunnel was built *C. G. Maggs*

15 The bleeding heart

In the 1960s it was possible to travel by rail from Wrexham to Swansea. A similar trip can be made today, but the route has seen many changes, the most significant being the loss of the many connecting lines. Much of the trip in the 1960s would have been on the 95½-mile Central Wales line, from Craven Arms & Stokesay to Swansea Victoria, which was a lengthy incursion by the former London and North Western Railway (LNWR) into South Wales. The company took control of the line in 1873 and constructed the Victoria terminus at Swansea in 1882. The LNWR did much to develop both freight and passenger services and the line continued to be busy in LMS days.

Nevertheless, since World War 2, with its traffic declining and crossing a very thinly populated area, there have been regular calls for closure of the Central Wales line. I have heard it said that on one occasion, very many years ago, when a decision to close the line was being considered, a map of mar-

ginal parliamentary constituencies along the route was examined. The line remains open against all odds to this day. It has, however, been cut from all its connecting passenger lines. The 6½-mile Pantyffynnon to Brynamman branch closed in August 1958, the 60-mile line from Moat Lane Junction through Builth Road Low Level to Three Cocks Junction and Brecon closed at the end of December 1962 and the 13½-mile line from Llandilo to Carmarthen closed in September 1963. The direct 12½-mile line from Swansea Victoria to Pontardulais closed in June 1964, Swansea trains being diverted via Llanelli. In August 1964 the Central Wales line itself closed for through freight.

Below: 'Black 5' 4-6-0 No 45406 heads the last booked passenger train out of Swansea Victoria, the 18.25 to York on 13 June 1964. G. T. Robinson

Left: Pontardulais station building shorn of its canopies and where lines once ran to Swansea, viewed in July 1969. Author

Below: 2-6-0 No 46516 on the 1.20 pm Brecon to Moat Lane waits at Builth Road Low Level for a connection with the 12.20 pm Swansea Victoria to Shrewsbury headed by Class 8F 2-8-0 No 48354 in August 1962. B. J. Ashworth

Above: Builth Road in rather less pristine condition on
5 August 1967. Author

Right: Pantyffynnon station where the lines on the right once
provided passenger services to Brynamman, viewed in
August 1969. Author

Below: The Heart of Wales line was cut in October 1987 at a
river bridge south of Llangadog, but services were restored
and more happily the line still survives. T. Clift

ALL UP GOODS AND MINERAL TRAINS
MUST STOP DEAD HERE

Above: Pantydwr summit looking north on the Mid Wales line, after track lifting but still with the signs and signals. A. Muckley

Left: Llanidloes looking north in September 1963 with demolition in progress. A. Muckley

Above right: Plenty of freight activity on the WR line to the rear of Exchange station when this photograph was taken in the 1960s. C. Gifford

Right: Distinctly less freight activity on 20 August 1977. L. Bertram

Above: Ex-GWR 2-6-2T No 5572 arrives at Llangollen from Berwyn on 20 August 1988. One day the train may once again proceed right through to Ruabon. B. Dobbs.

An interesting trip is recorded on the line:

SATURDAY 5 AUGUST 1967; At Craven Arms the train stopped whilst the guard changed the points behind us. The line has been singled. The guard had GWR buttons on his coat and did not charge me extra to go to Llanbister Road where I found many soggy railway documents. On the return to Wrexham I could see that the line to Oswestry had only just been closed while that to Llangollen is still open for specials.

The Central Wales line has now been renamed the Heart of Wales line; it is still open from Craven Arms to Llanelli and is well worth a visit, but let us hope that

the many cuts will not lead to its bleeding to death. Llangollen has reopened, albeit westward towards Corwen, but one day it may again be possible to catch one of those specials from Ruabon!

The return to Wrexham was also of interest. The Welsh border market town was by the 1850s the heart of both coal mining and iron manufacturing industries. The parish church contains the tomb of Elihu Yale, the founder of Yale University. Wrexham General was once an important station on the GWR's Paddington to Birkenhead route. Through trains ceased in the 1960s and freight was withdrawn in the 1970s, but local services still use the station. General station is not the only one in the town. The Wrexham, Mold and Connah's Quay Railway opened its original station at Wrexham in 1886. An addition took its tracks beneath the GWR line to terminate in the town centre where a new Central station was opened in 1887. The earlier station was then named Exchange, but its services have since been linked into General station and Exchange no longer appears in timetables.

16 Blaenrhondda and a bus to Bridgend

The South Wales coalfield was famous for both the quality and the variety of its coals. The area has seen triumph and tragedy, prosperity and poverty, railway lines come and go. Before World War 1 South Wales was the largest coal exporting area in the world, there being hundreds of collieries employing thousands of men. In their heyday the railways conveyed enormous quantities of coal and other minerals from the valleys to the coast for export and to domestic markets elsewhere in Britain.

The first high pressure steam locomotive was used by Richard Trevithick in the Merthyr area as far back as 1804. In the many boom years that followed, competing lines ran up the valleys and beside industrially blackened rivers such as the Taff whose waters were used for coal washing. As prices rose, other fuels were used and new world sources of coal competed with South Wales. The 1920s saw shrinking exports and the coalfield in decline, together with its iron, steel and railway industries. In the 1960s the railway system contracted and lines were lost at an unprecedented rate. The decline in coal freight still continues and no fewer than 48 of the 59 branch lines existing in the South Wales area in 1967 had closed by 1993. However, on the passenger side a turning point was reached in the mid 1980s after which usage increased and the decline was at last halted.

Although much is being done to heal the scars of industrialization, evidence of the decline exists in almost every valley. An interesting area is found near

Above: A typical Welsh coalmine near Crynant, but open in 1993 only as a tourist attraction. Author

Left: The decline of the South Wales Coalfield. This sad museum piece photographed in September 1993 speaks for itself. By April 1994 only one British Coal pit remained. Author

Great Western Railway

WHOM do YOU SERVE?

GREAT WESTERN RAILWAY.

The Agreement of Service provides that each man will "abstain from any act that may injuriously affect the interests of the Company" and that "seven days' previous notice in writing of termination of service shall be given."

NOTICE TO THE STAFF.

The National Union of Railwaymen have intimated that railwaymen have been asked to strike without notice tomorrow night. Each Great Western man has to decide his course of action, but I appeal to all of you to hesitate before you break your contracts of service with the old Company, before you inflict grave injury upon the Railway Industry, and before you arouse ill feeling in the Railway service which will take years to remove.

Railway Companies and Railwaymen have demonstrated that they can settle their disputes by direct negotiations. The Mining Industry should be advised to do the same.

Remember that your means of living and your personal interests are involved, and that Great Western men are trusted to be loyal to their conditions of service in the same manner as they expect the Company to carry out their obligations and agreements.

Felix J. C. Pole,
General Manager.

Paddington Station,
May 2nd, 1926.

THE NATIONAL UNION OF RAILWAYMEN.

Unity House,
Euston Road,
London, N.W. 1,
May 1st, 1926.

MINERS' CRISIS.

Arising out of the dispute in the Coal Industry this Union in common with others affiliated to the Trades Union Congress has agreed to give its support to the Miners during the present lockout and further, in accordance with the decision arrived at, at a Conference of Trades Union Executive Committees convened by the General Council of the Trades Union Congress, it has been agreed to take steps, in conjunction with the Transport Workers Unions, to call upon our members to cease work on Monday next, the 3rd instant.

I am conveying this intimation to you in order that you may be cognisant of the fact that in ceasing work the men are acting upon the instructions of the National Union of Railwaymen.

C. T. Cramp.

Unity House,
Euston Road,
London, N.W.1,
5th May, 1926.

MINERS' CRISIS.

I desire to repeat on behalf of the N.U.R. what I said in yesterday's issue of the BRITISH WORKER

Members of our Union must handle no traffic of any kind, Food-stuffs or otherwise.

C. T. Cramp.
National Union of Railwaymen.

Left: NRM Poster. Industrial relations were not always harmonious

Below: In wintry conditions on 29 January 1978, having run around their train to the north of Treherbert station, Class 20 Nos 20142 and 20030 prepare to couple up for the return to Cardiff. J. Chalcraft

Centre right: In the mountains above Blaenrhondda, even in 1993 the remains of an old boiler associated with mineral activity in the area could still be found. Author

Below right: Trevithick's tunnel at Merthyr in September 1993. It was here in 1804 that the first high pressure locomotive successfully hauled a train loaded with bar iron. Author

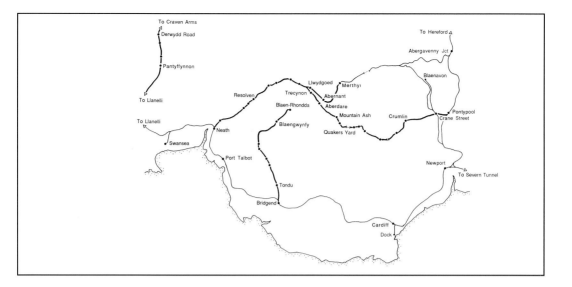

Blaenrhondda. The Rhondda and Swansea Bay Railway (R&SBR) connected with the Taff Vale Railway line north of Treherbert. In joining the Rhondda with the Avon Valley to draw upon this once flourishing mining district the R&SBR was forced to construct the longest tunnel in South Wales, the 1mile 1,683yd Rhondda Tunnel. The construction work took in excess of three years and the tunnel was finally opened in July 1890, thus providing a line via Cymmer and Tondu from Bridgend to Treherbert. In November 1960 this line was blocked when a runaway unfitted freight train collided head on with a passenger train below Cymmer. A longer albeit temporary closure resulted at the end of February 1968 due to geological movement in the tunnel and the section between Cymmer and Treherbert had a bus substituted for the train service. Apparently this was not made entirely clear to the intending passenger!

The diary states:

22 JULY 1969: A very wet day. The trip to Treherbert was a bit of a disaster. I set off late and the bus got jammed and I had to run all the way from Cardiff Castle to General Station. I just caught the train, but there was no toilet and I sat almost bursting all the way up the valley. When I arrived at Treherbert and asked where the train to Bridgend was they said 'they don't run through the tunnel any more, but you can get a bus'. A bus indeed, no one had said the line was closed, I therefore returned to Cardiff with my mission unaccomplished.

Initially there were difficulties in substituting bus services in this rugged area, but rail services finally succumbed to this type of transport in June 1970. Today the tunnel has been sealed and at

Left: Troedyrhiew Garth station looking south on 16 October 1971 after passenger services had ceased. *A. Muckley*

Below: Single carriage on the Bridgend to Treherbert line at Nantyffyllon on 17 April 1968. *C. Gifford*

Right: Map of Blaenrhondda 1921. *Crown Copyright*

Below right: Tondu station, east side, looking north in October 1971. *A. Muckley*

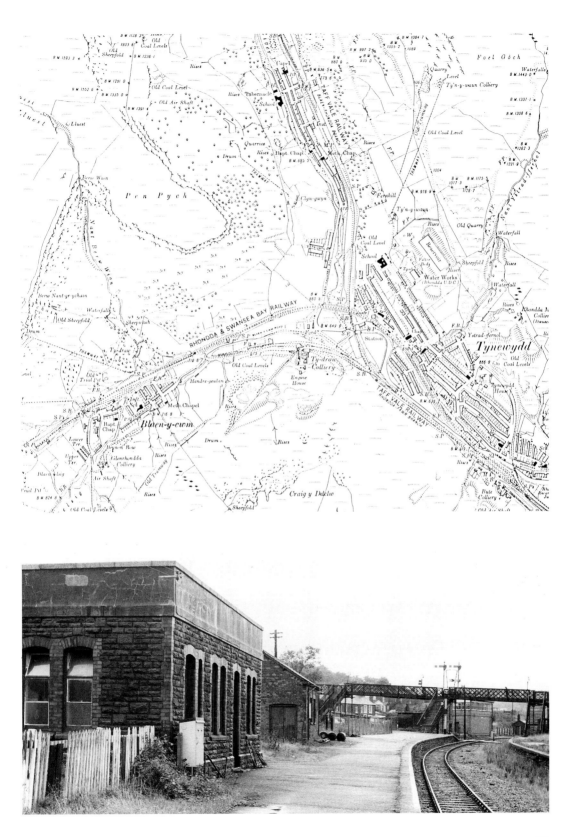

Blaenrhondda only a manhole betrays its original portal. None the less much still remains in the area as a reminder of past industrialization, including the odd rusting boiler high up the valley side at Blaenrhondda. Finally, passenger trains still run south from Treherbert station to Cardiff.

Above: Caerau station looking north on 16 October 1971 after passenger services had ceased. A. Muckley

Right: The enforced closure of the Rhondda Tunnel meant that the 'terminus' of passenger services from Bridgend was Cymmer Afan. Of note is the modern signalbox and the old Swansea Bay line on the left. This scene was taken in April 1970, two months before the line finally succumbed to closure of normal passenger services on 22 June 1970. J. Vaughan

17 Neath to Pontypool via Crumlin

The history of the former GWR routes from Neath to Merthyr Tydfil and to Pontypool Road is essentially one of two separate lines that joined in the middle. The line from Neath to Pontypool and its section to Merthyr contained some of the most magnificent engineering works in Wales. The lines conveyed massive quantities of coal in their time, but in passenger terms just imagine what a uniquely spectacular panoramic cross-section through South Wales the 41½-mile Neath to Pontypool line would have provided!

The western section was the first to open, in September 1851, from Neath to Aberdare. The Vale of Neath Railway (VNR) built a line via the Vale of Neath to a junction west of Hirwaun where one branch ran to Merthyr Tydfil and the other to Aberdare. The railway had associations with the GWR from the beginning and, since Brunel assisted as engineer, it was a broad gauge railway.

At the eastern end of the line the Newport, Abergavenny and Hereford Railway (NA&HR) opened a line from Pontypool Road to the east side of the

Right: Neath Riverside station looking north towards Glyn Neath and the main Swansea to Cardiff line on 18 May 1958.
N. C. Simmons

Below: Class 37 No 37220 heading an empty coal train past the remains of Neath Riverside station and about to pass under the main line on 9 September 1977 on its way up the Vale of Neath.
L. Bertram

Above: Maintenance work being undertaken during the summer of 1993 at Resolven to restore freight services on the Neath to Aberpergwm section of the Neath to Pontypool line. R. Trill

Above: Looking north at Resolven on a section of the Neath to Pontypool line that has since reopened. The bridge in the foreground carries a stream over the railway. R. Trill

Below: Hirwaun station in September 1962 looking towards Merthyr. A. Muckley

Above: Llwydcoed on the Merthyr section looking towards Merthyr in September 1962. *A. Muckley.*

Below: Hirwaun station in September 1993. The line was still used for freight from Tower colliery, the last British Coal deep mine in South Wales which closed in 1994. *Author*

Crumlin Viaduct in August 1855. The short but expensive section over the Crumlin Viaduct was opened in June 1857 from Crumlin to Pontllanfraith. The last stretch built by the NA&HR, to Quakers Yard, opened in January 1858.

The concept of connecting the two lines was reinforced when they were taken over by the GWR in 1863. The route was soon continued from Quakers Yard through the Duffryn Tunnel to join the Vale of Neath Railway at Middle Duffryn Junction almost exactly midway between Pontypool Road and Neath. In order to enable through running, a third rail was added on the VNR section and from 1865 the whole route between Pontypool and Neath was worked as part of the GWR.

The western section included a line to Merthyr which crossed under the mountains dividing the Afon Cynon from the River Taff via the 1mile 737yd Merthyr Tunnel, the third longest in Wales. This tunnel proved burdensome and construction took some six years. The line to Merthyr Tydfil did not open until November 1853, by which time much of the industry in the area was already on the wane. At this time the town, once the largest in South Wales, was also in decline.

On the eastern section of the line was one of the most sensational engineering works in the Western Region. The Crumlin Viaduct was designed by C. Liddell and built by T. Kennard. It was of straight-forward construction which, with its slender iron open lattice work, gave it particular elegance. It had a length of 1,656ft and a height of over 200ft above the Ebbw Vale at its highest point, making it one of the greatest viaducts of its kind in the world. It required more maintenance than some stone viaducts and in

the late 1920s the GWR were forced to re-deck the viaduct, replacing iron plates with steel. Furthermore, to reduce stress on the viaduct, both set of tracks were realigned to the centre, thus ensuring that only one train at a time could cross the structure.

For many years the Neath to Pontypool line acted as a trunk freight route across the coalfield, although passenger use was essentially local in nature. In the

Above: 0-6-2T No 6664 soon after leaving Hengoed High Level station and crossing Maesycwmmer viaduct with the 7.45 am Aberdare to Pontypool Road train. The line in the foreground was the Newport to Brecon route. W. G. Sumner

Below: A daring last view from Crumlin Viaduct taken in April 1965 before its demolition. P. Hocquard

Above: A three-coach train crossing the Crumlin Viaduct. D.Lawrence

Below: View from the remaining section of Crumlin Viaduct, September 1993. R. Trill

Below: One of the two remaining stone abutments at either end of the former Crumlin Viaduct, September 1993. R. Trill

end the line's destiny was linked to that of the mines along its route and in the area. As these declined so did the revenue on the line. The whole route closed to passengers in June 1964, thus losing, probably for ever, a unique panoramic journey through South Wales.

The great Crumlin Viaduct was reduced to scrap during 1965, although viewing platforms have been constructed on the remaining stone piers at either end. A little further west, although unused, the stone-arched Maesycwmmer viaduct has survived. A number of individual sections remained open to serve collieries on the line, but the section from Pontypool to Hafodyrynys closed in 1979. The section from

Nelson to Treharris was in situ in 1993, although unused since the closure of Deep Navigation Mine in 1991. Plans have been considered for the reopening of this section to passengers, but as yet have come to nothing. Today the simplified track work at the former Pontypool Road station is a far cry from the days of a substantial station and its sidings. Yet not all is lost; the line from Neath to the north of Resolven has reopened for freight traffic for the Cwmgwrach coal disposal point. The section from Tower Colliery through Hirwaun and on to the Cynon Valley line at Aberdare also remains in use for freight, with plans for possible passenger reopening to Hirwaun being considered.

95

18 Chard Central

Being at a watershed, rain falling at Chard may eventually run either to the Bristol Channel, or to the English Channel, depending on which side of the main street it drops. A similar situation existed at Chard station with trains in one direction being run by the GWR and those in the other by the L&SWR. For many years the two companies employed separate staff and signalling at the station.

The earliest railway to serve Chard was the Chard Railway which linked the town some 3¼ miles south to the L&SWR main line. Opening in May 1863, the com-

pany almost at once became part of the L&SWR and built the line to standard gauge. However, the Chard and Taunton Railway's 15-mile connection to the GWR main line at Taunton via Ilminster provided a useful second route to the town. Part of this route used the general course of an earlier waterway and was opened as a broad gauge line in September 1866 to a new joint station at Chard. The red brick and stone station had only one through platform. It was built in a combination of styles, but has a superb overall roof supported by a brick colonnade. The whole building has a hand-

Left: A quiet moment in the station approach at Chard Central in June 1962. R. C. Riley

Below left: Continuing quiet at Chard Central in September 1993. Author

Right: 0-6-0PT No 9670 on Chard Junction train in Chard Central station on 14 June 1962. R. C. Riley

Below: Chard Central station in use as a garage in September 1993. Author

some and balanced appearance. The station was run by the GWR from 1876. The L&SWR reached the joint station, or Central station as it later became known, shortly after, by the construction of a direct extension from its own line. Through running was not feasible to Taunton until the GWR line was modified to standard gauge in 1891.

The L&SWR Chard Town station closed to

Left: 0-6-0PT No 4663 takes water at Chard Central on 7 May 1960. J. C. Haydon

Below left: 0-6-0PT No 4663 arrives at Chard Central with the 2.50 pm train from Taunton on 7 May 1960. J. C. Haydon

Above: 2-6-2T No 5571 on the 2.50 pm Taunton to Chard Central restarting from Donyatt Halt on 1 September 1961. M. J. Fox

Below: 0-6-0PT No 4612 on the 2.50 pm Taunton to Chard branch train leaving Ilminster. R. E. Toop

passengers as far back as January 1917, although it was retained until the mid 1960s for goods. Trains were diverted to Chard Central and worked through to the L&SWR main line by the GWR. During World War 2 the D-Day landings were planned from near Ilminster. With the exception of a short section at Chard Junction the line became part of the WR. The line through Chard was closed temporarily to passengers during a fuel crisis of 1951. Although called Central station it was not very centrally located in the town and the station and lines to it closed to passenger services in September 1962, whilst freight lingered on for a couple more years. Central station, which is a listed building, remains and is in use as a garage.

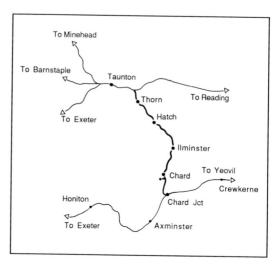

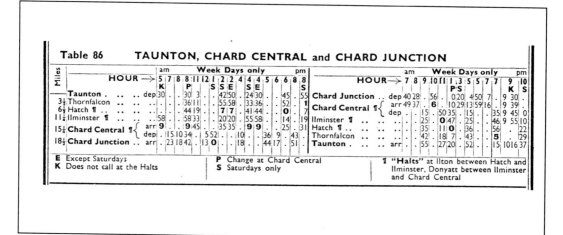

Table 86   TAUNTON, CHARD CENTRAL and CHARD JUNCTION

Miles	HOUR →	am 5 7 8 8 11 12	Week Days only 1 2 4 4 4 5 6 6 8 8	pm	
		K	P	S S E	S E	S
—	**Taunton** .. .. dep	30 .. .. 30 3	.. 42 50 .. 24 30 .. .. 45 .. 55		
3½	Thornfalcon	.. .. .. 36 11	.. 55 58 .. 33 36 .. 52 .. 1		
6½	Hatch ¶	.. .. .. 44 19	.. 7 7 .. 41 44 .. .. 0 .. 7		
11¼	Ilminster ¶	.. 58 .. 58 33	.. 20 20 .. 55 58 .. .. 14 .. 19		
15¼	**Chard Central** ¶ { arr	9 .. .. 9 45	.. 35 35 .. 9 9 .. .. 25 .. 31		
	dep	.. 15 10 34 .. 5 52	.. .. 10 .. .. 36 9 .. 43 ..		
18¼	**Chard Junction** .. arr	.. 23 18 42 .. 13 0	.. .. 18 .. .. 44 17 .. 51 ..		

HOUR →	am 7 8 9 10 11	Week Days only 1 3 5 5 7 7	pm 9 10	
		P S	K S
Chard Junction .. dep	40 28 .. 56 ..	0 20 4 50 7 .. 9 30 ..	
Chard Central ¶ { arr	49 37 .. 6 ..	10 29 13 59 16 .. 9 39 ..	
dep	.. .. 15 .. 50 35	.. 15 .. 35 9 45 0	
Ilminster ¶	.. .. 25 .. 0 47	.. 25 .. 46 9 55 10	
Hatch ¶	.. .. 35 .. 1 0	.. 36 .. 56 .. 22	
Thornfalcon	.. .. 42 .. 18 7	.. 43 .. 5 .. 29	
Taunton .. .. arr	.. .. 55 .. 27 20	.. 52 .. 15 10 16 37	

E Except Saturdays	**P** Change at Chard Central	¶ "Halts" at Ilton between Hatch and
K Does not call at the Halts	**S** Saturdays only	Ilminster, Donyatt between Ilminster and Chard Central

Left: Emerging from Hatch Tunnel 0-6-0PT No 3736 with the 8.0am from Taunton to Chard on 31 August 1962. The tunnel was originally built to accommodate double track broad gauge lines. *R. G. Turner*

Above: July 1955 timetable.

19 A Wessex terminal

The Bridport Railway ran some 9¼ miles over the South Dorset Downs from Maiden Newton, on the River Frome, via Toller and Powerstock to Bridport on the River Brit in this attractive area of Wessex. The line opened as far as Bridport in November 1857 and in March 1884 was extended a further 2 miles to Bridport Harbour, which was renamed West Bay. The line, almost from its opening, was a subsidiary of the GWR and until 1871 ran as a broad gauge route.

Left: Station sign at Maiden Newton. G. Beale

Below: The 12.42 pm Bridport to Maiden Newton train formed by a single unit, W55035, arrives at Toller on 23 April 1975, two weeks before closure. The buildings have since been moved to Totnes. G. F. Gillham

Bridport harbour's commercial trade contributed little revenue to the line as the general prosperity of established industries in this locality declined. It was therefore hoped that renaming the harbour West Bay would boost tourism and that the locality might indeed challenge other major seaside resorts. Some speculative work commenced on a promenade, but tourism failed to develop as expected. Although it was

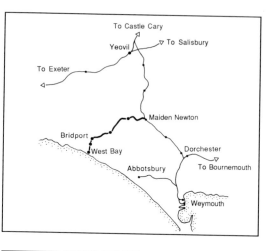

Left: A single railcar awaits at the gas-lit Bridport station on 13 July 1970 having formed the 13.20 from Maiden Newton. J. H. Bird

Below: Bridport station; a quiet moment on 11 August 1966. Author

Right: Ivatt 2-6-2T No 41320 climbs out of Bridport, banked by another 2-6-2T on the return leg of the LCGB 'Bridport Belle' railtour from Waterloo on 22 January 1967. P. Claxton

an attractive part of Wessex, the shingle waterfront and the infrequent and indirect train service could not compete with other south coast destinations. Hardy's *Far From the Madding Crowd* was usually more the order of the day!

Thus it was that the short line to West Bay was an early casualty. It had temporarily closed for passengers during World War 1, but closed permanently for passengers in September 1930, although freight continued to use the line until December 1962. In contrast, the line to Bridport appeared to have survived the Beeching cuts of the 1960s. Whilst freight traffic to Bridport ceased in June 1965, economies had been made and even when closure was proposed, extensive

objections were lodged. It looked as if the line might not become a lost line. Unfortunately, after a number of reprieves, the line finally closed in May 1975.

My diary states one of the problems of the line:

It is a devil to get to anywhere from Bridport station. Just to go to Taunton you have to go 40 miles from Castle Cary to Westbury and back!

The station buildings at Bridport have long since been demolished, but those from Toller have been reassembled on the South Devon Railway near Totnes.

The Tivvy Bumper Service

The line from Taunton to Exeter via Tiverton Road opened in 1844 as part of the Bristol and Exeter Railway. It was built to broad gauge, as was the 4¾-mile branch from Tiverton Road running westward to the town of Tiverton which opened in June 1848. On the opening of the branch, Tiverton Road station was renamed Tiverton Junction. The line was converted to

Left: Class 47 No 47493 passes Tiverton Junction on 16 July 1976 with the 12.12 Paddington to Penzance train. Although closed the platforms remained in situ in 1993. B. Morrison

Right: 0-4-2T No 1450 propelling the 15.11 auto train out of Tiverton towards Tiverton Junction on 18 August 1964. I. Holt

Below: 0-4-2T No 1450 and auto train at Tiverton on 26 September 1964. M. J. Fox

Below right: With the exception of this bridge, very little remains on the former site of Tiverton station; much of the land was being used for a new road when this view was taken in September 1993. Author

standard gauge in June 1884 when a splendid new stone station was opened at Tiverton to connect with the 25-mile Exe Valley line, which ran from Stoke Canon on the main line just north-east of Exeter, to Morebath Junction south-east of Dulverton. Although forming a more direct route to Exeter than that via Tiverton Junction, this direct line through Tiverton from Exeter to Dulverton closed in October 1963.

The single line from Tiverton Junction to Tiverton ran a shuttle service to connect with both main line trains and Exe Valley trains. The push-pull trains on the line were known as the 'Tivvy Bumper' service. The one halt on the line, at Halberton, was opened in 1927. Passenger services on the line to Tiverton were withdrawn, without producing any discernible economies, in October 1964, and freight was with-

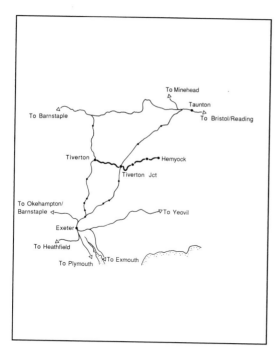

drawn in June 1967. Tiverton Junction station closed in May 1986 when a new park-and-ride station was opened called Tiverton Parkway. By 1993 little trace remained of Tiverton station whilst Tiverton Junction remained derelict, but with its platforms largely intact.

The Farmer's Line

Running eastward some 7¼ miles from Tiverton Junction to Hemyock, in the upper reaches of the Culm Valley, was the appropriately named Culm Valley Light Railway. Rather like the Channel Tunnel, it cost more to build than estimated and also opened later than anticipated, in May 1876. Here I hope comparison ends, as traffic did not meet expectations and

Right: Unlike passengers, milk cannot be kept waiting too long and the line provided a seven day service for this freight. 0-4-2T No 1462 on the Sunday milk train for Hemyock trundles into Uffculme on 2 August 1959. *D. Fereday Glenn*

Below right: 0-4-2T No 1442 with a train for Tiverton Junction at Culmstock on 13 April 1963. *R. N. Joanes*

Below: Map of Tiverton 1906. *Crown Copyright*

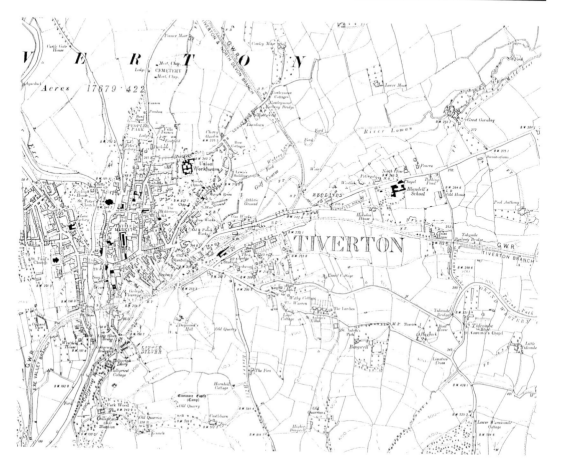

Left: Culmstock station sign, white lettering on blue patent enamel, preserved at Tiverton Museum in 1993. *Author*

Below: Tranquil rural scene at Hemyock as the driver reads the paper, and more cows than passengers are to be seen. *Ian Allan Library*

Right: The ground frame from Hemyock is preserved at the railway museum at Swindon, June 1993. *Author*

Far right: Hemyock station sign together with other articles from closed lines in the area are preserved at Tiverton Museum. *Author*

Below right: July 1955 timetables.

the shareholders, many of whom were local farmers, agreed to sell out to the GWR in 1880. The line ran without major incident; indeed the trains ran so sluggishly that there were problems in employing dynamos to work electric lights in the coaches. Passenger trains were withdrawn from the three stations and two halts in September 1963. Freight, particularly in the form of milk traffic from the Hemyock creamery, continued until 1976. The ground frame from Hemyock is preserved at Swindon Railway Museum, whilst two of the line's small 0-4-2 tank engines, Nos 1442 and 1450, have also been preserved. The railway gallery at Tiverton Museum contains many relics of the lines in the area.

Table 83 — TIVERTON JUNCTION and HEMYOCK (Third class only)

Miles		am	am	am	pm	pm	pm	pm			Miles		am	am	pm	pm	pm	pm	pm
					E		S								E		S		
—	Tiverton Junction.. dep	8 45	1135	1135	4 0	4 30	5 0	7 5	.		—	Hemyock .. .. .. dep	7 20	1030	..	..	3	0 5	5 5	7 55
2¼	Coldharbour Halt	8 54	1144	1144	4 48	4 38	5 8	7 14	.		1	Whitehall Halt	7 24	1034	....	..	3	5 6	0 8	0
2¾	Uffculme	8 57	1147	1147	4 52	4 42	5 12	7 17	.		2¼	Culmstock	7 31	1043	..	1210	3	13 6	8 8	7
5	Culmstock	9 21	..	12 52	4 4	4 52	5 22	7 27	...		4½	Uffculme	7 40	1053	1210	1219	3	25 6	18 8	17
6¼	Whitehall Halt	9 30	..	..	2 13	5 0	5 30	7 35	.		5¼	Coldharbour Halt ..	7 43	1057	1218	1223	3	30 6	22 8	20
7½	Hemyock .... arr	9 42	....	....	2 20	5 5	5 35	7 40	...		7½	Tiverton Junction.. arr	7 52	11 7	1228	1233	3	41 6	33 8	29

E Except Saturdays.   S Saturdays only.

Tables W 85 to W 88

Table 85 — TIVERTON JUNCTION and TIVERTON—(Third class only)

Miles		am					Week Days						pm		am				Week Days							pm	Sun
	HOUR →	7	8	8	9	9	1011	121	2,4	5	5	7	8	9	HOUR →	7	7	8	9	1012	1	2	4	4	6	8	9	9	10	8
			A	S	E	B	T		E	D	E	S					H	H	J		E		B				J	S		pm
	Tiverton Junc. dep	25	15	50	2	40	35 25	.	50	40	22	25	6 30	5 40 25	Tiverton . .. dep	10	40	45	20	55	20	20	0	0	45	25	15	0	L45 20	8L50
2½	Halberton Halt ..	31	20	55	7	45	40 30	.	55	45	27	30	11 35	10 45 30	Halberton Halt ..	17	47	51	26	1	26	26	6	6	51	31	21	6	L51 26	8L56
4½	Tiverton . .. arr	38	27	2	14	52	47 37	.	2	52	34	37	18 42	17 52 37	Tiverton Junc. arr	23	53	57	32	7	32	32	12	12	57	37	27	12	L57 32	9L 2

A 5 minutes *earlier* on Saturdays	E Except Saturdays	L Through Train to Exeter (Table 87)
B 10 minutes *earlier* on Saturdays	H 15 minutes *earlier* on Saturdays	S Saturdays only
D 7 minutes *earlier* on Saturdays	J 10 minutes *later* on Saturdays	T Tuesdays only

21 **Disappearing Dartmoor**

The spectacular moorland of Dartmoor with its tors of bare granite crowning the upland and its picturesque valleys makes it an appealing tourist area. Its natural resources include granite, which resulted in the construction of some of the earliest tramways for its transportation. The area is not heavily populated and experiences severe weather. Sir Arthur Conan Doyle described it as 'a great place, very sad

Far left: One of the earliest tramways in this area brought granite down from Haytor which can be seen in the distance. Trucks were guided by grooves in the granite sets. Parts of the line were still visible in 1993. *Author*

Left: The Ashburton terminus of the branch from Totnes was secured by the Dart Valley Railway and for a time the station was used to store rolling stock. *Ian Allan Library*

Below left: This view from within Ashburton station, taken in April 1971, highlights what an attractive preserved terminus it would have made. *A. Muckley*

Right: The interior of Ashburton station in September 1993. Although mutilated by garage use, the basic structure remains intact. *Author*

Centre: The line from Totnes remains open and is now run by the South Devon Railway Trust as far as Buckfastleigh, where this view from the signalbox looking towards Ashburton and with 0-4-2T No 1420 in sight was taken in July 1970. *J. M. Boyes*

Below: The original signalbox remains at Buckfastleigh in 1993, but since the line to Ashburton was cut by a road scheme it has not been in regular use and has been replaced by a new box to the south. *Author*

and wild'. Sherlock Holmes arrived here by train in 1902 to solve the case of The Hound of the Baskervilles unaware that future dark and dastardly deeds would be done to the railways in the area!

Ashburton *(The case of the truncated terminus)*

The first aim of the Buckfastleigh, Totnes and South Devon Railway was to build a line from Totnes up the Dart Valley as far as Buckfastleigh. Nevertheless, agreement was reached for a continuation of the line to Ashburton, a Stannary town due to its trade in tin, and at the heart of the remaining wool trade in the district. The 9½-mile broad gauge line opened in May 1872 and was amalgamated with the GWR in 1897. The line never made a notable financial return, although Ashburton fair days contributed significant freight to the wider network. It was closed to passengers in November 1958 and for freight in September 1962.

Left: Freight at Heathfield station; a view looking towards Newton Abbot on 28 February 1959. M. Windeatt

Above: 2-6-2T No 4547 looking particularly smart at Bovey in the 1950s. D. Sellman

Below left: After closure to passengers Heathfield station fell into disrepair. E. Francis

This was not the end, however, but the beginning of a new chapter. The track remained *in situ* and the Dart Valley Railway Company reopened the line as far as Buckfastleigh in 1969. Unfortunately, the section beyond Buckfastleigh to Ashburton was required for a new section of the A38 road. A one day valedictory passenger service was run over this overgrown section in October 1971 just before it was ripped up. The South Devon Railway Trust which took over the line from the Dart Valley Railway continue to run the line, which follows the River Dart through 7 miles of delightful Devon countryside from Totnes to its terminus at Buckfastleigh. Most of the section beyond Buckfastleigh to Ashburton is now roadway, whilst Ashburton station is in use as a garage.

Moretonhampstead
(The station for Baskerville Hall)
The Moretonhampstead terminus at the end of the 12-mile branch from Newton Abbot, as in the case of Ashburton, also boasted an overall Brunel roof. The Moretonhampstead and South Devon Railway's broad

gauge line up the Bovey Valley and its tributary was opened in July 1866. Between Teigngrace and Bovey it used part of the route of an old granite tramway which was opened in 1820 to bring granite down from quarries at Haytor until its closure in 1858. This earlier lost line was unique in that it used granite blocks which were cut with grooves to allow flangeless wagon wheels.

Moretonhampstead could never boast a frequent service, although it is said that an open wagon was sometimes run down the valley to Bovey after the last train had left for the benefit of late night revellers! After various plans to extend the line by means of a light railway to Chagford were abandoned, in 1906 the GWR began running buses to that village. The railway also provided a connecting service at Moretonhampstead to their hotel. As with the Buckfastleigh line there was tourist potential, but in spite of this the line closed to passengers in March 1959. The section above Bovey was closed to all traffic in 1964 and the track was cut back to Heathfield after a special one day final service of passenger trains in 1971.

Left: Bovey station in September 1993 remained largely intact, although the railway tracks had been replaced by a road. R. Trill

Centre left: Bovey station sign, white letters on blue enamel, preserved at Didcot Railway Centre. Author

Below left: Pullabrook Halt (formerly Hawkmoor) was the shortest platform on the branch. This view taken on 28 February 1959 is looking towards Moretonhampstead. M. Windeatt

Below: Moretonhampstead 'up' starter on 14 February 1959. The lattice post signal was a comparatively rare feature on the GWR. M. Windeatt

Above: 0-4-2T No 1466 at the Moretonhampstead terminus. D. Lawrence

Left: The sad sight of Moretonhampstead station in July 1964. A. Muckley

Above left: Many of the buildings remained at Moretonhampstead in 1993, including the old engine shed, although the overall station roof has long since gone and the site is used as a road transport depot. Author

Above: The gates to Moretonhampstead station, September 1993. Author

Left: Although tableware and other items at the Manor House Hotel are no longer GWR embossed, a number of GWR features remain such as this fire hydrant in the car park. Author

Moretonhampstead retains some of its railway buildings including the engine shed, the station being used as a road transport depot.

Moretonhampstead also retains an important link to the GWR: its fine Jacobean-styled Manor House Hotel, built in 1907. This dignified building in its landscaped grounds was designed by the architect Walter E. Mills. Originally built for the 2nd Viscount Hambledon, whose father William Henry Smith is best remembered as the founder of W. H. Smith the stationers, it was sold to the GWR in 1929, who subsequently developed the property as an hotel. Guests arriving by rail were transported along the narrow Devon lanes in the hotel's taxi. In 1935/6 the building was sympathetically extended. It was requisitioned in

Top: The Manor House Hotel remains in use as a hotel in 1993. Author

Above: Moretonhampstead station was linked to the Manor House Hotel in GWR days via a taxi, or rather executive mini bus service. Ian Allan Library

both World Wars, nationalised in 1948 and sold into private ownership in 1983. In 1932 the hotel was used as Baskerville Hall in the film *The Hound of the Baskervilles*. The building remains in use as an hotel.

Princetown (*A danger of snakes*)

Princetown was named after the Prince of Wales, who became George IV in 1820. The isolated Dartmoor town, which is nearly 1,400ft above sea level, had become the site of the Napoleonic Dartmoor Prison completed in 1809. The 10½-mile Princetown Railway line from Yelverton to Princetown, opened in August 1883, snaked its way upward to what became the highest GWR station in England. The line followed in part the abandoned route of the earlier Plymouth and Dartmoor line. Much of the early traffic was associated with the prison, but King Tor quarry also provided some granite as freight. Later on tourism was the main trade as this line was one of the most scenic sections of railway in England. Ingra Tor Halt, one of three halts on the line, was famous for its notice which warned alighting passengers with dogs of the likely presence of snakes. The unique sign is restored in a museum at Plymouth. The line closed in March 1956 and was dismantled by the following year. The weather on the last day conspired to blanket the moors with mist. Only a solitary building remains on the site of Princetown station, but much of the route across the moors can still be clearly traced.

Left: NRM Poster. GWR hotel posters of the time were all of similar design.

Below left: 2-6-2T Nos 4568 and 4583 haul the 2.51 pm Yelverton to Princetown train, seen here leaving Burrator Halt on 3 March 1956. *S. C. Nash*

Below: The bleak King Tor granite quarries, disused in 1953. *M. E. Ware*

G. W. R.
(W. & S. Ltd.)

Moretonhampstead

G. W. R.

Ashburton

22 Plymouth and Launceston

The South Devon and Tavistock Railway linked Plymouth with Tavistock by a 13-mile line which ran northward via Yelverton, skirting the edge of Dartmoor. The line opened in June 1859.

Subsequently the Launceston and South Devon Railway extended the line westward over the upper reaches of the Rivers Tavy and Tamar some 19 miles into Cornwall and to Launceston. The extension was

Left: Yelverton on 15 July 1965. The Princetown branch platform to the left of the view is already somewhat overgrown. R. C. Riley

Below: 2-6-2T No 5572 on a Plymouth to Tavistock single coach auto train at Marsh Mills on 29 August 1961. The Plym Valley Railway is dedicated to restore services from this station some 1½ miles north to Plym Bridge. R. C. Riley

Right: Auto-trailer W226W and 0-4-2T No 1434 on 12.35 pm auto train to Plymouth at Tavistock South on 5 June 1959. J. H. Aston

Below: Tavistock South station unused in June 1966. It has since been completely demolished. A. Muckley

officially opened on 1 June 1865, which turned out to be a day of unprecedented rainfall, and 'railway weather' became a local expression taken to mean wet weather. It was a broad gauge line and soon became part of the GWR. The line was converted to standard gauge in 1892.

This GWR line was well used up to World War 2 by tourists to this attractive area, but soon after a decline set in. By the late 1950s, particularly in the winter months, trains were carrying very few passengers. There was also a duplication of lines serving the area. From Plymouth as far as Lydford, where the former L&SWR station had been built alongside the GWR station, the GWR line was duplicated by the Southern's

main line. The companies also had two stations side by side at Launceston. A World War 2 connection had been made in September 1943 between the town's SR and GWR stations. This later enabled train services to be concentrated at the Southern station, and the WR station closed in June 1952.

The entire line from Plymouth to Launceston was to close at the end of December 1962, but the weather on closure, as with the opening, was severe. The night of 29 December coincided with an unprecedented blizzard and the last passenger trains could not run. The weather on that occasion reinforced the local expression 'railway weather'. The Lydford to Launceston section was reopened for freight in 1964,

but the (ex-GWR) Tavistock to Lydford section closed the same year. The remaining freight services from Lydford to Launceston ceased in February 1966 and much of the track between Launceston and Tavistock was removed the same year. Today much evidence of the line has disappeared, including the station buildings at Tavistock South, Lydford, Lifton and Launceston, together with the viaduct at Walkham and many bridges. Indeed at Lydford an ancient footpath known as 'The Way of the Dead' leads to the church. Yet the abandoned station and overgrown line here could well compete for such a title. In spite of all the foregoing closures, at Launceston a narrow gauge steam railway was opened in 1983 and runs from a new station located broadly to the west of the old ones.

Above: The 10.15 am Launceston to Plymouth train leaving Lydford in April 1961. M. J. Esau

Centre: Lydford station buildings have all been demolished and the site was very heavily overgrown in September 1993. R. Trill

Right: Lifton station in the 1950s. The design is similar to Bovey station. D. Lawrence

Left: 0-6-0PT No 4679 with a Launceston to Plymouth passenger train arriving at Lifton on 9 July 1960. Hugh Davies

Above: The general area of former station at Launceston. A solitary GWR signal still remains in 1994. Author

Below: Steam at Launceston in 1993. Just west of the old GWR station the Launceston Steam Railway runs along the old L&SWR route. Author.

23 GWR: God's wonderful railway

The Latin words above the fireplace in the former GWR hotel at Moretonhampstead read: Deo Non Fortuna Fretus. This translated means 'Relying On God, Not On Fortune'. The words are not without some relevance to the GWR. It was perhaps no accident that the GWR museum at Swindon was housed in a former religious building, as it was said that whilst Paddington answered to Swindon, Swindon answered to God. GWR trains, hauled by engines named after saints, ran to cathedral cities, and clerics were to be found amongst its passengers. Yet the accolade of 'God's Wonderful Railway' was earned only after many years. Before the Severn Tunnel was completed, you will recall, the initials GWR were sometimes unkindly referred to as meaning the 'Great Way Round'. Other expressions have also been derived from the initials, but in later years it became

Right: The sun sets on a GWR lamp at Didcot Railway Museum. Author

Below: The former Wesleyan chapel and now a railway museum at Swindon. City of Truro being winched into the building at 11.25 am on 5 April 1962. M. Pope

increasingly difficult to deny the railway God's own title.

The esteem in which the GWR is held by so many is, in part, due to the facts that the Great Western had both a particularly distinctive corporate image, that was designed to impress, and that the company was extant for over a century. The sheer magnificence of the engines, the image of great engineering works, the glamour, tradition and style created over these years was even carried through to the Western Region, which at first went out of its way to reflect its past traditions. Even after later attempts to obliterate the past, it is still possible to stumble upon heart-warming examples of the GWR company, almost half a century after its demise, not just at one of the many preserved railways, but more often continuing in active service.

I leave you with the following thought. Someone recently said to me: ' 'Tis a fine day, 'tis the GWR, 'tis paradise.' I contemplated the remarks; lost lines or not, clearly 'God's Wonderful Railway' is immortal !

Above: GWR Monogram. *Ian Allan Library*

Below: The GWR lives on: new parts for GW engines are forged at the Didcot Railway Centre. *Ian Allan Library*